"To the Uttermost of My Power"

The Life and Times of Sir William Pepperrell

1696 –1759

Richard A. Brayall

HERITAGE BOOKS
2008

HERITAGE BOOKS
AN IMPRINT OF HERITAGE BOOKS, INC.

Books, CDs, and more—Worldwide

For our listing of thousands of titles see our website
at
www.HeritageBooks.com

Published 2008 by
HERITAGE BOOKS, INC.
Publishing Division
100 Railroad Ave. #104
Westminster, Maryland 21157

Copyright © 2008 Richard A. Brayall

Cover illustration: William Pepperrell. Engraving by J. Rogers. Opposite page 151 of *Life of George Washington*, [extra illustrated edition], volume 1, part 1, by Washington Irving. New York: G. P. Putnam & Co., 1857-59
Courtesy of the Massachusetts Historical Society

All rights reserved. No part of this book may be reproduced or transmitted in any form or by any means, electronic or mechanical, including photocopying, recording or by any information storage and retrieval system without written permission from the author, except for the inclusion of brief quotations in a review.

International Standard Book Numbers
Paperbound: 978-0-7884-4634-4
Clothbound: 978-0-7884-7179-7

"To The Uttermost Of My Power"

This book was type set using
Microsoft Word for Windows
In Bookman Old Style
9 and 11 point.

Bookman Old Style is a serif
typeface developed by
Alexander Phemester in 1860.
It been updated three times
since its inception.

"TO THE UTTERMOST OF MY POWER"

DEDICATION

FOR MY WIFE DANITA
SONS AARON, TREVOR AND SPENCER
DAUGHTER-IN-LAW JULIE
GRANDDAUGHTER NORA
AND GRAM AND GRAMP

"To The Uttermost Of My Power"

CONTENTS

Illustrations	vii
Acknowledgements	viii
Preface	xi
Prologue	xiii
Pepperrell And The King	1
Roots Along The Piscataqua	12
The Pepperrell Enterprise	25
Under New Management	33
The Frontier On Fire	50
Louisbourg	64
"A Mad Scheme"	72
New England Unites	85
New England Has Arrived	98
The Siege Of Louisbourg	104
Dissention In Command	119
"The Happy Issue"	126
"To The Uttermost..."	141
A Return Triumphant	155
"Hold Fire!"	161
A Great Bereavement	177
"The Old French War"	194
A Life With Honor	210
Last Will And Testament	218
The Fate Of The Family	222
The Passings Of The Era	229
A True New England Hero	231
Select Bibliography	238
Index	244

"TO THE UTTERMOST OF MY POWER"

Illustrations

1. SIR WILLIAM PEPPERRELL AS COLONEL OF THE 51ST REGIMENT
2. THE PEPPERRELL MANSION TODAY
3. THE LADY PEPPERRELL HOUSE
4. THE FIRST CONGREGATIONAL CHURCH
5. A BRIGANTINE, THE WORK HORSE OF THE FAMILY FLEET
6. KITTERY POINT, MAINE, ROAD SIGN
7. THE WHITE BLOCKHOUSE OF FT. MCCLARY OVERLOOKING PEPPERRELL COVE AND THE PISCATAQUA
8. KITTERY POINT FROM KITTERY, LOOKING OVER SPRUCE CREEK
9. A RIVER OF BRIDGES

All photography by Trevor Brayall

"To The Uttermost Of My Power"

Acknowledgements

Pepperrell researchers are fortunate that a large number of the family records were saved and archived and are still in good condition. Having been confined to a wheelchair for the last two years due to an accident that ruined my left knee, I have been unable to get to various places to do the research needed for such a book. I wish to thank the Massachusetts Historical Society in Boston for giving me access to their collection of Pepperrell papers and the William Shirley papers through their online catalog, copying the material and then sending it to me. That was a life-saver, because no writer wishing to understand the Baronet can do so without their help.

Thanks again to the Massachusetts Historical Society for permission to quote from a number of documents and letters that are in their custodial care. Other key sources, i.e., Parkman and Parsons, are in the public domain and need no such approval.

Another institution useful and helpful to me was the Portsmouth, NH, Public Library. I thank the staff for their help with Pepperrell and with his old friend, Governor Benning Wentworth, as well as providing document copies for me.

Other organizations that provided guidance and assistance were the New Hampshire Historical Society in Concord, New Hampshire, and The Peabody-Essex Museum in Salem, Massachusetts.

During my research, I found two secondary sources that are essential for any work being done on Sir William Pepperrell. His 19th century biographer -- Usher Parsons -- prepared his book as a precious combination of narrative and primary sources. Modern writers have been critical of Parsons for his historical "method," and they may be correct, but I still found his preservation of letters and documents very useful. For while Parsons does write some prose about the Baronet, he also includes some very important original documents from Pepperrell's life, including letters and other items. For years, this book was out of print, but the University of Michigan Press has brought it back to life.

The second source can be summed up in two words: Francis Parkman. No one can write knowledgeably about the French and Indian Wars without reference to the Boston historian's monumental *History of France and England in North America*. Even though most of this seven-volume history is more than a century old, the writing is

"TO THE UTTERMOST OF MY POWER"

still fresh and invigorating. His understanding and description of the Louisbourg campaign in *A Half Century of Conflict* is essential for anyone wishing to know about and understand "the mad scheme."

The other authors include Canadian J.S. McClennan, whose *Louisbourg: From Its Foundation to Its Fall* is simply a wonderful and readable look at the short-lived French fortress. Finally Neil Rolde's 1982 *Sir William Pepperrell of Colonial New England* is a well-written, highly detailed road map of the Baronet's fascinating life and times.

I have limited the use of footnoting for one major reason -- or two if you include saving my sanity. Too many notes and citations are, in my humble opinion, too distracting for the reader, and sometimes the citations are redundant or add nothing to the story. Any factual information a note might have provided, I tried to include in the text itself.

The most important thanks has to go to the people at Heritage Books for taking a chance on an unknown writer with, I think, a good idea. It is a scary prospect to write a manuscript of more than 60,000 words and then to have no place to send it. That was where things stood with this book. All I had to show for all that work was a growing pile of rejections until Leslie Wolfinger of Heritage Books said "yes." She made a dream come true.

I also thank my family for putting up with a writer doing his first book and for reading the chapters as I spit them out. No matter what I said about your criticism, I didn't mean it.

Special thanks go to my mother-in-law, Mrs. Nadean Cercone of Kittery, who served as my chief copy editor and proofreader. Thanks for his profound patience go to my father-in-law, her husband Tony. Also grateful thanks to my wife Danita, my oldest son Aaron and his wife Julie, who read through each version looking for the inevitable errors and typos. I'm sure their newborn daughter Nora read some too.

Thanks also to my sons Trevor and Spencer for listening to my ideas during some late night Red Sox games, and for telling me when they were good and when they were not so good. Trevor also handled the photography. Their help truly made this a real family affair.

Finally, I wish to thank my maternal grandparents, the late Harry and Charlotte Whenal of Kittery, Maine, who brought me up in that charming coastal town. Luckily for me, they attended Kittery Point's

"To The Uttermost Of My Power"

First Congregational Church where I first heard stories about Sir William Pepperrell. I also thank my grandmother for instilling a love of learning and history in me. I only wish she could have seen this book.

All mistakes, omissions, and misinterpretations belong to me.

RAB

"To The Uttermost Of My Power"

Preface

IF NOT FOR THE ACCIDENTS OF HISTORY OR THE VAGARIES OF BIRTH, THE COMMANDING GENERAL OF THE AMERICAN REVOLUTION'S CONTINENTAL ARMY COULD HAVE BEEN A RESIDENT OF THE DISTRICT OF MAINE -- THEN PART OF THE COLONY OF MASSACHUSETTS. IN ANOTHER TWIST OF FATE, THE "MOUNT VERNON" OF THE UNITED STATES MIGHT TODAY BE LOCATED ON THE PISCATAQUA, NOT THE POTOMAC, RIVER.

The rebellious American colonies did not have a strong military tradition in 1776. Yes, there were militia and "minute men" organizations, but they were highly unreliable and it would take years for those armed volunteers to coalesce into an effective fighting force. For decades, the Provincials had depended on the hated "redcoats" or "lobster backs" to protect them from their French and Indian foes.

It was no secret that George Washington's military experience in the French and Indian War was limited and quite unremarkable. So who did have that background? Who had that competency of command?

William Pepperrell did. But due to one of those historical accidents, he also had been dead for 17 years in 1776.

People don't remember William Pepperrell today, but when he died in 1759 at his home in Kittery Point, Maine, he was one of the richest men in the colonies; he was a leader in the Massachusetts legislature; he was a

"TO THE UTTERMOST OF MY POWER"

lieutenant general in the British Army; and he was the first American to become a baronet. He earned that distinction by commanding the "New England Land Forces" that captured France's Louisbourg fortress on Cape Breton Island in 1745. That victory was the only major military action undertaken by the British during King George's War in North America, and Pepperrell was the commanding general. George Washington was an admirer.

But by 1776, Pepperrell was dead. He never had the chance to try the Revolution on for size. But he was a man who helped make those colonies safe and made it possible for them to give birth to the American Revolution and the entire American experience.

His life is the story of a simple son of a simple fisherman, who took what he was given, and through luck, determination and talent, made himself into a colonial aristocrat and a New England hero.

Sandown, NH   July 6, 2007

"To The Uttermost Of My Power"

Prologue

For the close observer, the Pepperrell name begins to pop up once you enter Kittery Point.

Even the road notes the difference, as its name changes from Whipple Road to Pepperrell Road halfway across the relatively new bridge spanning Spruce Creek. This swirling bit of tidal water also divides Kittery, Maine, from the section of the town known as Kittery Point.

The road itself honors the two Williams who rose to prominence in the Kittery of the mid-eighteenth century. Whipple Road honors William Whipple, a merchant from the Maine town who represented New Hampshire at the Second Continental Congress and who signed the Declaration of Independence. Kittery Point's Pepperrell Road is named for, of course, Sir William Pepperrell.

For those who don't know, Kittery is the very first town in Maine if you enter the state from the south. It is also the state's oldest incorporated town, dating back to 1647. Even though the outlet malls invaded years ago, it is still a pleasant, quaint community. But in many ways it is a town still in search of an identity even if it is more than 350 years old.

Its location is most of its problem. The town sits on the north -- the Maine -- shore of the Piscataqua River, directly across from Portsmouth, New Hampshire. The Portsmouth Naval Shipyard, the region's largest employer, is totally within the geographic boundaries of the town -- you can't get to it unless you go through

"TO THE UTTERMOST OF MY POWER"

Kittery -- yet it has always carried the name of the larger city across the river.

The river itself is an obstacle. One of the swiftest flowing waterways in the world, the 12-mile long river is formed by the confluence of the Salmon Falls and the Cocheco Rivers, and forms part of the boundary between the states of Maine and New Hampshire. For centuries, the currents did not lend themselves to an easy crossing or to bridges. That has changed today -- now three well-used highway bridges span the water to link the towns and the states. But 300 years ago, the river was a major obstacle.

For Kittery residents, the majority of their interests lay to the south -- in Portsmouth and Hampton, New Hampshire, and northern Massachusetts. After all, it is less than 100 miles to Boston. People work in that direction, where the good jobs are. But governmentally, Kittery belongs to Augusta, 106 miles to the north.

Once in Kittery Point, the Pepperrell name becomes more and more prominent. There is Pepperrell Road itself; then the Lady Pepperrell House, a restored 18th century home built for Sir William's widow after his death. The house is close to the cemetery of the First Congregational Church -- the oldest in the state of Maine -- and the house and the cemetery property sit on a riverfront lot overlooking the Portsmouth Naval Shipyard.

Just a bit down the road, you come to Pepperrell Cove, a large inlet of the Piscataqua River. Today that cove is dotted with a large number of moored sail and motorboats for those local residents lucky enough to be waterborne, or for the annual influx of summer tourists. At one time, if I remember correctly, there was also a Pepperrell Cove Water-skiing Club that used to perform

"To The Uttermost Of My Power"

in the cold waters of the inlet, but I am not sure it even exists anymore.

Hidden near an equally historic grocery store and a wall along the road, is the real treasure. It is what appears to be a large, rambling, expanded homestead that is in fact the former home of the real Sir William Pepperrell. It is a private home today and, like the Lady Pepperrell house, it is not open to the public.

There it sits, hundreds of years after the death of its famous owner, a brooding presence behind its wall, testimony to the strength and wealth of the man who conquered the most formidable fortress in North America during King George's War.

It does not sit alone in its antiquity, for just up the road is the Bray House, thought to be the oldest home in Maine. It was the dwelling of Margery Bray, the mother of Sir William.

But just who was William Pepperrell? What did he do to be remembered? Exactly what era did he live in? I imagine few people today who live in Kittery can identify him, except noting that he was the man for whom much is named.

But why was he so honored by the citizens of his colony?

He was the son of a successful merchant who built his father's mercantile business from the coast of Maine into a financial empire whose tentacles reached into the four corners of the known business world.

He was a citizen soldier who helped to raise colonial fighting forces to oppose the French in North America

"TO THE UTTERMOST OF MY POWER"

and was rewarded with the command of a regiment and, eventually, much more.

He was, for a time, the strong ally of Massachusetts Governor William Shirley, who gave him the opportunity for heroism and then became jealous of his success.

He was in charge of the largest single military operation the English undertook during King George's War in America and he carried it out successfully.

It also appears that his fellow soldiers, as well as his business customers and his neighbors in Kittery and Maine, genuinely liked him. It is hard to find a negative comment about Pepperrell in any documentary sources, and his reputation as a loving husband and parent remains unsullied.

Because of the success of the Louisbourg expedition, Pepperrell received some key royal awards from King George II. He was the first colonial citizen to be raised to a baronet from any British North American colony, and he remained a loyal British citizen for the rest of his life.

Pepperrell was of the generation preceding that which fomented and successfully fought the American Revolution. Pepperrell was dead well before the Stamp Act began to awaken thoughts of independence among the American colonists.

As a result, Pepperrell was a true colonial figure, having been born and having died under the rule of the British crown. It is hard to imagine him encouraging a revolt against the King, but, in truth, it was hard to imagine many of our founding fathers doing the same.

"To The Uttermost Of My Power"

But even today his name resonates in the world of American business and advertising. West Point Pepperrell and "Lady Pepperrell" remain well-respected names in the textile industry. Both names are derived from the Pepperrell Corporation, a textile company founded on Pepperrell land in Saco, Maine, once owned by Sir William.

But why should we, in the 21st century, still want to know about Sir William Pepperrell? Well, for a number of reasons. First of all, the story of his family's business success is an inspirational tale and an example of how people could rise to unexpected stations in colonial America.

His life also shows Pepperrell as a true citizen soldier, one who used his prestige, power and persistence to reach an amazing goal in the defense of his fellow citizens.

Examining his life is also a way to personify important events in early American history and understand their impact on the colonies and their citizens.

Finally, it is a fascinating and exciting story to tell.

"To The Uttermost Of My Power"

Chapter I

Pepperrell And The King

WILLIAM PEPPERRELL, WEALTHY MERCHANT AND SUCCESSFUL "AMATEUR" GENERAL FROM KITTERY IN THE REMOTE BRITISH colonial district of Massachusetts called Maine, was 52 years old when he made his first and only trip to London in 1749.

After all the years spent growing his father's business into a trading monolith and after all the ships he had sent to sea, he had never once before made the transatlantic crossing.

Now he intended to make the best of his time in England. During his visit to the Mother Country, he would go to Devonshire and visit Tavistock, the village near Plymouth that was his father's birthplace. He would take a side trip to the home of Admiral Sir Peter Warren, his naval partner in the assault on the French fortress of Louisbourg. He would also play host to Warren in London, when the Admiral came to see him and while they checked over accounts from the Louisbourg venture so the colonies could be reimbursed by Parliament for their war expenses.

Most importantly, he would have an audience with the King, George II, ruler of Great Britain, Ireland and -- in ancient title only -- France, as well as possessions in the Holy Roman Empire.

Pepperrell had been known as Sir William since 1745 when the King conferred the baronetcy on him as a reward for leading the successful New England effort at the siege of Louisbourg.

2

"To The Uttermost Of My Power"

Physically, Pepperrell seemed to be a well-proportioned man, probably about 5 feet, 10 inches tall, and just a little overweight with an early "spare tire" beginning to show under his red frock coat.

Based on the portrait of Pepperrell by John Smibert -- the best-known contemporary artist in all the colonies[1] -- he has a long, honest face, naturally crinkled in a smile as he greeted friends from everywhere. Like many men of that time, he seems comfortable in his traditional white curly wig that he probably got up every morning to powder. Those wigs were not very becoming . . . unless they happened to hide a receding hairline, but there is no indication Pepperrell was doing that. He wore the wig because it was the style of the times and he was a stylish man.

There is no doubt he was a friendly man; someone could not be as popular as Pepperrell was unless he was an outgoing, engaging individual -- doubtlessly not an extravert or an introvert, but probably somewhere comfortably in between. He certainly seemed to be an unforgettable personality.

Unfortunately, almost all of the documentation from his visit -- letters, notes, diaries -- have been lost so we can only use informed conjecture to recreate his meeting with George II.

On the morning of the Royal audience, Sir William arose early at the London home of his friend and English fiscal agent, Christopher Kilby, and prepared for his meeting with the King. There is no record of where the King held

---

[1] "William Pepperrell" by John Smibert, is in the collection of The Peabody-Essex Museum in Salem, Massachusetts.

"To The Uttermost Of My Power"

this audience, but it could be assumed that since the meeting took place in London, the location probably was Whitehall Palace on the banks of the fabled river Thames. But it could have been at any of the many royal palaces or houses in the London area.

Since his arrival in London, however, Pepperrell had quickly become a veteran of the city's social reception circuit. The Lord Mayor had already received Pepperrell, and he had honored the Baronet with a double-handled silver cup commemorating the victory at Louisbourg. The Kittery man also had a long and interesting dinner discussing a wide range of colonial matters with General James Oglethorpe, the founder of the colony of Georgia and the conqueror of part of Spanish Florida a decade earlier. Pepperrell had also been feted and lionized by a variety of clubs and organizations throughout the city, being noted as a true military expert who had performed a miracle.

The Baronet also had an invitation to the court of Frederick, the Prince of Wales, who was estranged from his father, the King. The King and his heir literally could not stand the sight of each other and they established competing courts in the city. Frederick died before George II and never reigned; his son did, as George III.

THE DOORS TO LONDON SOCIETY OPENED TO PEPPERRELL BECAUSE OF HIS BARONETCY, which made him one of the most prominent and honored British subjects in North America. It put him in the august company of all British colonial governors as well as any of the generals or admirals who would command the red-coated soldiers and sailors in the continuing struggle with France for supremacy on the North American continent.

4

"TO THE UTTERMOST OF MY POWER"

Unfortunately history does not record the words that passed between Pepperrell and George II. But we can imagine what it was like when he approached the King in the crowded palace that day in London in 1749.

We can imagine that he walked up to the King wearing the large white wig that was so stylish in London society. His frock coat was probably red; no doubt to remind King George and his courtiers that Pepperrell had won these honors due to his military prowess. His legs were covered in white linen and the silver buckles shone brightly on his highly polished black shoes.

Nearing the King, Pepperrell no doubt kept his eyes low and bowed to his monarch and the other members of the nobility that made up the King's entourage. He bowed slightly before the sovereign, and then knelt on one knee. A courtier announced him to the King; George II probably nodded, smiled, looked directly at Pepperrell and spoke in Germanic-accented English.

We do know that the King asked Pepperrell what more the Motherland could do to protect the colonial frontier in America. Apparently the Baronet made several suggestions on ways to better protect the colonial fishing fleets around the Grand Banks. He did, however, avoid criticizing the Treaty of Aix-La-Chappelle. This treaty, which ended The War of the Austrian Succession and its North American counterpart, King George's War, had done the unthinkable -- it had returned the fortress of Louisbourg to the French. Pepperrell knew this was neither the time nor the place to discuss that turbulent question with the King.

Minutes later, Pepperrell had probably bowed again and moved along, his time with the King over. During their few moments together, His Majesty had given Pepperrell

"To The Uttermost Of My Power"

a carved wooden snuffbox with a portrait of Alexander the Great rendered in bas-relief on the cover. But now his part in the ceremony was done and Pepperrell went back to his small group of friends who had accompanied him to the palace.

One friend who was in London at the time and who went to the palace with him was Samuel Waldo[2], the New England merchant who had been one of Pepperrell's brigadier generals at Louisbourg.

Waldo was a life-long friend and contemporary of William Pepperrell. The son of Boston merchant Jonathan Waldo, he lived primarily in Falmouth, now Portland, Maine, because of the family's extensive land holdings in the Penobscot River area. He and Pepperrell had served together on the Massachusetts Governor's Council for many years.

It also seemed the two were destined to become even closer. Pepperrell's son, Andrew, had announced his engagement to Waldo's daughter, Hannah, shortly after he had graduated from Harvard College more than four years ago.

---

[2] Both men were born within days of each other in 1696, sons of New England merchants who inherited their fathers' businesses. Waldo spent much of his time in "down east" Maine, living in Falmouth, which would later be renamed Portland. Pepperrell shuttled between Kittery and Boston. They both served on the colony's Governor's Council, and, if Pepperrell had had his way, Waldo would have been second-in-command at Louisbourg. The two also went to their grave at the same time. Pepperrell lay ill in 1759, when in May of that year Waldo escorted Governor Thomas Pownall to the Penobscot area of Maine. There, he suddenly took sick and, without warning, died. Pepperrell himself would pass away just two months later.

"To The Uttermost Of My Power"

No doubt the two friends discussed the increasingly complex wedding situation. More than four years had passed since Andrew and Hannah announced their betrothal, but still no ceremony had taken place. The two families had endured two postponements, but they were losing patience. Especially Waldo, who was only looking out for his daughter's reputation in an era when reputation meant everything. Neither man could understand what was causing the delay in the nuptials. The problem was baffling to both men. It must have made the old friends uncomfortable.

In spite of the challenges he faced in his business, Pepperrell was becoming more and more comfortable in the role of being a baronet. He knew it was a special title, and he was proud of the work that had earned it.

A BARONETCY -- THE TITLE IS USUALLY ABBREVIATED AS BART. -- IS AN HONORARY POSITION IN the nobility of Great Britain that ranks just above that of a knight and below that of a baron. After baron, other titles are viscount, earl, marques and duke. Duke ranks just below prince of the realm.

King James I introduced the concept of the baronetcy in 1611 as a way to increase revenue for the Crown. There is no equivalent to a baronetcy in other European nations, although hereditary knights such as the German and Austrian *ritter* and the Dutch *erfridder*, apparently are similar.

Since the honor is hereditary, a baronetcy can be passed on to another family member. It is not, however, considered part of the British peerage and does not entitle the holder to a seat in the House of Lords, the now-powerless upper house of Parliament. In addition, while the holder of a baronetcy is called "sir," it is not

"To The Uttermost Of My Power"

considered a knighthood since it outranks all other knighthoods except the orders of the Garter and of the Thistle.

Sir William Pepperrell, Bart., the victor at Louisbourg, fully aware of his place in the aristocracy, might have looked back and wondered how this unremarkable little man who barely spoke English ever obtained the throne of his country.

In 1688, England's Glorious Revolution replaced the unpopular Stuart King, James II, with the tandem of his eldest daughter, Mary, and her husband, Prince William of Orange, from the Netherlands. William and Mary jointly ruled England until Mary died of smallpox in 1694, and William became the sole ruler.

King William died in 1702 and the throne passed to Mary's surviving sister, Anne. Queen Anne ruled until 1714 when she too passed away. Despite the fact that Anne had endured 17 pregnancies during her lifetime, she had no living children at the time of her death. Her dynasty -- the Royal Stuarts of the Restoration of Charles II -- was at its end.

Several years before Queen Anne's death, the rules for succession had changed. The Act of Union, which combined the Kingdoms of England and Scotland into Great Britain in 1707, contained a provision requiring all monarchs to be Protestant. That cut the list of possible successors to the throne down to one -- a German prince, George, the Elector of Hanover. This hereditary ruler was one of five such "electors" from throughout Germany, whose primary function was to "elect" the Holy Roman Emperor. George was also the duke of Brunswick-Luneberg, the great-grandson of James I, the

"To The Uttermost Of My Power"

first Stuart King, and a nephew of Queen Anne. His mother, in fact, would have succeeded to the throne had she not died shortly before Queen Anne.

This obscure prince was crowned George I, King of Great Britain, on October 20, 1714, at Westminster Abbey in London. George preferred his German possessions to England, and during his reign he spent much of his time tending to his continental holdings. He also spoke English poorly and generally used German or French during public ceremonies. Not especially popular with his English subjects, he was known throughout the country as "German George."

During the latter part of his reign, he spent more and more time in Germany and took little interest in English matters. He let his ministers handle affairs on the island, especially Sir Robert Walpole, who became his "prime" minister and who made many of the policy decisions for the nation.

On June 27, 1727, King George I died. The throne of England went to his eldest son, who was crowned George II. This George paid much more attention to English affairs and even made the effort to become fluent in the language. He also was the last English monarch to lead troops in time of war, taking part in several European battles won by the famous Duke of Marlborough. This duke, born John Churchill, was one of the pre-eminent military leaders of his day; Sir Winston S. Churchill was a direct descendant.

Before his ascension to the throne, George II had had a nasty, adversarial relationship with his father, who for some reason despised his only son. They couldn't stand each other, they rarely spoke, and, when they did, they

"To The Uttermost Of My Power"

could not agree on anything. The Prince of Wales even set up his own court in an attempt to outdo his father.

As time passed, George II, like his father, became less and less interested in the affairs of the British Isles, and he too delegated more royal power to his prime minister and other cabinet members. By the end of the reign of George II's grandson, George III, most royal power was to be permanently in the hands of the prime minister and cabinet through Great Britain's unwritten constitution.

Traditionally, Great Britain played a minor role in European affairs, since the island nation had no continental possessions to protect and often found comfort behind the treacherous waves of the English Channel.

But when the Hanoverians came to the throne, they brought a substantial continental bias with them. To the first two Georges, France under Louis XIV and Louis XV, was the great evil who threatened their German possessions. As a result, England found herself entangled in diplomatic and military alliances with allies such as Austria and Prussia in hopes to foil French ambitions for European dominance. As a result, Great Britain took part in more and more Continental wars, such as the Wars of the Spanish and Austrian successions.

AS SIR WILLIAM LEFT THE PALACE, AFTER HIS AUDIENCE WITH GEORGE, the second Hanoverian King, he must have marveled that he, the son of a simple fisherman, had just had an audience with the monarch of Great Britain. Pepperrell well knew that this would have never happened if he had been living in England. In "the Mother Country", everything was based on your social

"To The Uttermost Of My Power"

class. But the colonies were different. There, it was not who you were, but what you did that mattered. That is why Pepperrell was treated almost like a lord. It must have made him proud to be an American on a day he would surely never forget.

We do know he enjoyed visiting his father's former home in the Plymouth area, where he met a number of relatives with whom he corresponded until his death. We do know that he truly enjoyed his reunions with Admiral Peter Warren, the chief naval officer at Louisbourg and whose wife was a colonial from the DeLancey family of New York. We know he brought a pair of black thoroughbred horses home with him, a gift from Admiral Warren to the colony of Massachusetts. We know that the ship he boarded was a swift schooner owned by his company and managed and maintained by his son Andrew.

The ship left London on August 20, 1760.

Leaving in August meant that the ship would have to face the early part of the hurricane season in the Atlantic, but Pepperrell apparently felt it was worth the risk. He wanted to go home.

Forty-two days after leaving London, lookouts on the ship sighted the New England mainland. The captain skillfully skirted several small islands just off the coast of Maine, and then turned west into a broad, flat tidal estuary unlike most of the others in the region -- the Piscataqua River.

As the ship sailed up the river, it passed Fort William and Mary in Newcastle on the New Hampshire shore.

"To The Uttermost Of My Power"

Knowing who was on the vessel, the fort commander ordered an 11-gun salute to honor the returning baronet.

Sir William had been away for almost a year. He was glad to be home.

"To The Uttermost Of My Power"

Chapter II

Roots Along The Piscataqua

THE ISLES OF SHOALS SIT SOME NINE MILES OUT TO SEA FROM THE COMMUNITIES OF KITTERY, MAINE, AND PORTSMOUTH, NEW HAMPSHIRE.

Even today they are nine rocky, scrub-covered islands, mostly unpopulated and extremely desolate places, especially in winter.

The islands were discovered by Captain John Smith in 1603. Today, a church owns several of the islands and a hotel is usually open for tourists in the summer months on Star Island. They are not major tourist attractions. Appledore Island is home to an oceanographic station operated by Cornell University and the University of New Hampshire.

A Portsmouth-based nautical cruise line has a tour that explores the Isles of Shoals, and occasionally someone goes ashore. Many houses and buildings are shuttered and closed and boarded. No doubt the elements that rule the Isles will make short work of them in the years ahead. The names of some of the islands sound like they should be on beer labels rather than on navigation charts -- Appledore, Smuttynose, and Star.

Today, the Isles of Shoals have two major claims to fame -- the infamous pirate Blackbeard is rumored to have buried part of his treasure on Appledore Island, and in 1939, the submarine *U.S.S. Squalus* sank off the Isles of Shoals during sea trials. Part of the crew survived after using a revolutionary rescue system, and the submarine

"To The Uttermost Of My Power"

itself was raised and served in World War II as the *U.S.S. Sailfish*. Today the conning tower of the submarine is preserved as a memorial to submariners at the Portsmouth Naval Shipyard.

During the late 1600s, however, the Isles of Shoals was the center of a thriving offshore fishing industry. The sailors and fishermen would catch tons of the cod, bass and mackerel that teemed near the isles, bring them ashore, dry and salt them on the land, then load up their vessels and take the preserved fish to North American or European ports for sale. By 1675, this activity had been thriving for 50 years, and the European demand for fish was growing.

THAT SAME YEAR, A 24-YEAR-OLD SAILOR from the village of Tavistock -- also Sir Francis Drake's birthplace near Plymouth, Devonshire -- in England, arrived at Appledore Island to try and make his fortune. He was an experienced seaman and a veteran of the Grand Banks fishing fleet. His name was William Pepperrell.

Although the family had lived in Devonshire for several generations, the Pepperrell name is thought to be of Welsh derivation. It was spelled in several different ways until William brought the current form to the New World.

Unschooled and unlettered, Pepperrell nevertheless was ambitious and eager and he knew his way around ships and around fish. Before coming to the Isles of Shoals, he had spent several years working the fishing fleets off the banks around Newfoundland. Once he arrived in the Piscataqua area, Pepperrell went into a partnership with Ambrose Gibbons from Topsham, England, and for nearly five years they caught fish, dried and salted them,

"To The Uttermost Of My Power"

shipped them and sold them. They also made a special, lucrative type of cod called dunfish.

Dunfish is cod that is cured with less salt and for a longer period of time than regular salted cod, and that curing produces a more tender, tastier fish. It was highly prized in the seventeenth century.

As time went by, the partners came to own several small ships designed for transporting their cargo. Rather than sail them themselves, they instead would lease them to other traders or captains who would make the trading voyages in return for a percentage of the profits or take their own cargo.

In addition, Pepperrell also held shares in ships owned and operated by other merchants in the Piscataqua River area.

Family records indicate Pepperrell made only one voyage in a company ship when he was a passenger on the *Andrew and William* that made its way to and from the Dutch port of Rotterdam in 1705. Pepperrell kept in touch with his family back in England and even looked into buying an estate in Devonshire later in life, but he never returned to the Plymouth area.

After five years of working together, Ambrose Gibbons decided to move up the coast of Maine to what is now the Waldo County area. Pepperrell chose to stay along the Piscataqua and go into business for himself.

He also made another decision that had a major impact on his life and moved his home from the Isles of Shoals -- where today a plaque marks the location of his house on Appledore Island -- to the nearby settlement of

"To The Uttermost Of My Power"

Kittery, in the District of Maine, part of Massachusetts. No doubt young Pepperrell needed a more vibrant and active community than the fishy Isles of Shoals, but it is likely that Kittery had other attractions for him.

During his early years in the trade, Pepperrell had used the services and talents of a local Kittery Point tavern owner, ship's chandler and shipwright by the name of John Bray. Bray was a fellow countryman of Pepperrell's, having come from the Plymouth area in Devonshire as well. They struck up an ongoing friendship, even though Bray was much older than Pepperrell. Bray already had a family when he came to Kittery, and that family including a young daughter named Margery. By the time Pepperrell arrived, Margery was a flirtatious, lively young woman who certainly attracted Pepperrell's interest. Margery previously had been engaged to a local man, Joseph Pierce, who unfortunately had passed away before they could be wed. If Margery filled a void in Pepperrell's life, then he certainly filled one in hers.

Bray had been looking for an appropriate husband for Margery for some time, but with little luck. He liked Pepperrell well enough, but apparently he had some doubts about the man's ability to provide for his daughter. He wanted proof that Pepperrell would take care of Margery and any children they might have. To show Bray that he could, the young suitor loaded up a ship with fish, and sailed to Newfoundland to sell his cargo to French settlers there. Apparently he earned enough hard cash to satisfy the doubting father because in 1680 William Pepperrell married Margery Bray. The wedding was held in the front parlor of what today is known as the Bray House. The Pepperrells lived with the Brays for two years while William continued to establish

"To The Uttermost Of My Power"

his business and Margery began to produce a family. At the end of that two-year period, John Bray had purchased about ten acres of land adjacent to his property from a neighbor who happened to be leaving Kittery for what he hoped would be greener pastures. Bray gave a portion of that land to William and Margery, and Pepperrell began building a home. It was the beginning of the Pepperrell estate and the foundation of the family land empire.

The first installment of the Pepperrell home was a large, square two-story dwelling on land overlooking what would come to be called Pepperrell Cove. Unlike many of the more opulent homes across the river in Portsmouth, this house needed no "widow's walk", on the roof so the master or lady could pace around the roof while looking out to sea in search of missing sails.

Pepperrell's house was in such a location that he could look out any second story window and watch his ships enter and leave the mouth of the Piscataqua. The cove itself was well sheltered and could provide safety in any kind of weather.

Once the house was built, the couple moved in and continued to raise a family that eventually consisted of two boys and five girls. The first-born was a son named Andrew, after his grandfather, and he was to be the family heir. The second son born was named William after his father and, though no one knew it then, he was destined for future glory.

Life for the young Pepperrell family in colonial America was good, as it was for most people who had left their old existence behind in Europe. Land was generally available, unlike in Europe, and could be purchased

"To The Uttermost Of My Power"

easily. In England, one out of every ten people owned land; in New England, it was nine out of ten. Even if newcomers could not buy established property, they could go out into the uncharted woodlands to stake their own claim for a homestead.

Food was also plentiful and there was no reason for anyone to ever go hungry. The forests surrounding the settlements teemed with deer, rabbit, pheasant, quail, wild turkey, moose and bear, and a skilled hunter never let his table go empty.

Fish -- from both salt and fresh water -- was also a large part of the colonial menu, both fresh caught and salted and dried. Other food from the sea included clams, oysters, scallops, shrimp and that marvelous crustacean, the lobster. Lobsters were so plentiful in those days that they were considered to be food for company, or even for prisoners. Taverns in the region were stocked with lobsters that were boiled, broiled or baked and served with large dishes of fresh-churned melted butter. People were known to order them by the dozen. Other temptations included broiled haunches of venison, beef and mutton, served with fresh potatoes, corn, squash, beans and vegetables and fruits grown and harvested in the back yard. All of that could be washed down by a number of beverages, including in the right season, fresh-pressed apple cider.

Fresh-baked bread was a key part of their diet and on most Saturday nights, the Provincials sat down to dinners that consisted of hot baked beans that had cooked all day in brick ovens, accompanied by bread that had cooked along side the pie for the evening. Pie fillings embraced a wide variety of flavors from apple and blueberry to squash, pumpkin and custard.

"To The Uttermost Of My Power"

Beer, ale, wine and distilled spirits like whiskey and rum were cheap and generally available in a large number of taverns and inns that dotted the countryside and the roadways. In addition, a variety of punches and mixed drinks were available, and most of the local farmers raised the crops needed to brew their own beer and ale for family consumption.

It truly seemed like a land of plenty.

William Pepperrell also picked up a title during those years in Kittery. Eager to do their share to protect the settlements and their residents, he and John Bray joined the York County Militia. Eventually, he was chosen to head that unit as its colonel and that title stuck.

FIRST EXPLORED BY MARTIN PRING IN 1603, THE PISCATAQUA River region that was to be central to the Pepperrell family was not settled until around 1622. Most linguistic experts believe the name of the river is derived from the Abenaki Native American language and means a place where waters divide into more than one branch. That would describe this river since about 12 miles inland, the Piscataqua divides into the Cocheco and Salmon Falls rivers.

Kittery in these early days was in essence a series of small, interconnected villages that stretched along the river for nearly nine miles. These cluster villages -- Kittery Point, Kittery proper, Upper or North Kittery and so forth -- united and became incorporated as a single entity in 1647, making it the first town to be so organized.

Today, it is the oldest town in the State of Maine.

"To The Uttermost Of My Power"

The town took its unique name from the birthplace of Alexander Shapleigh, one of the town founders -- the manor of Kittery Court at Kingswear, Devonshire, England. Shapleigh arrived in the New World in 1634 aboard the ship *Benediction*, which he co-owned with another founding father of the town, Captain Francis Champernowne.

The original map of Kittery was much larger than today's. Three centuries ago, the town extended up the Piscataqua for miles to the Salmon Falls River, and it included all the land that would eventually create the Maine towns of Eliot, South Berwick, Berwick and North Berwick.

The north shore of the Piscataqua River -- and several islands in it -- proved to be an excellent location for shipbuilding and maintenance, soon shipyards and repair docks were dotting the shoreline as far up river as Great Bay. By 1700, more than 900 people lived in the settlement of Kittery. In 1723, there were nine towns in the district of Maine, and the largest community was still Kittery.

THE ROYAL CHARTERS FOR THE COLONIES OF MAINE AND NEW HAMPSHIRE ORIGINALLY WERE GRANTED BY THE CROWN TO SIR Fernando Gorges and John Mason, respectively.

Mason named his colony after Hampshire, which was his home region in the midlands of England. Gorges called his segment of the land grant "Maine," but the attribution is a bit more muddied. Some think it was a reference to the old province of Maine in France. But other historians feel the name may have come from the fact it was the "mainland" -- much the way the Spanish

"To The Uttermost Of My Power"

referred to their South American properties as the Spanish "main."

When Gorges -- the Lord Proprietor of Maine -- died in 1652, that thinly populated province became an administrative part of the Massachusetts Bay Colony. Maine remained a political unit of Massachusetts until 1820, when it was admitted to the Union as part of the Missouri Compromise.

Spreading along the south shore of the Piscataqua was the Crown Colony of New Hampshire, and the communities of New Castle and Portsmouth. First settled in 1630, Portsmouth was originally known as Strawbery Banke in honor of the wild strawberries that grew on the shore. When it was incorporated in 1637, the settlement's name was changed to Portsmouth.

For many years, Portsmouth was the capital of the New Hampshire colony, and it quickly surpassed Kittery as the political and socio-economic engine of the Piscataqua Region. As the colonies grew, Portsmouth became one of the leading ports along the eastern seaboard. It was the largest colonial port north of Boston, and the region served as a defensive buffer for the much more populated Massachusetts colony.

The twin settlements of Portsmouth and Kittery provide an interesting glimpse into colonial community development. No bridges spanned the swiftly flowing Piscataqua River, its currents and eddies threatening doom for those who didn't know its idiosyncrasies. Only rudimentary ferries or rental boats and canoes dared cross that current. The river had no fords.

"To The Uttermost Of My Power"

Portsmouth had developed as a centralized community, a city, with distinct commercial and residential districts. Kittery was more like a collection of farms and settlements, clustered around several small villages. The two communities were very different.

They grew differently because of the river.

When Portsmouth grew, it grew to the south and the west like the United States itself eventually would. Kittery would never benefit because the prosperity did not cross the river, which blocked the way south and the way west. Maine always grew slower in terms of business and industry because it could not follow the growth trends west.

In addition, Portsmouth was the provincial capital; Kittery was Boston's distant outpost; Portsmouth was Anglican; Kittery was Congregational; Portsmouth was aristocratic; Kittery was of the common man; Portsmouth was domesticated beef; Kittery was wild venison. The swirling river protected Portsmouth from attacks by the French and Indians to the north; with its back to the river, Kittery had nowhere to hide. What often interested Kittery, disinterested Portsmouth and vice versa; Kittery often resented its perceived second-class status; Portsmouth didn't care.

Langdon Towne, the main character in Kenneth Roberts' celebrated 1936 novel, *Northwest Passage*, was a fictional resident of Kittery in the 1750s. Roberts emphasized in great and amusing detail the dichotomy between Kittery and Portsmouth. In the novel, Towne becomes an artist and portraitist and is hired to paint studies of prominent local residents for the Warner

"To The Uttermost Of My Power"

family to display in their Portsmouth home. One of the portraits he paints is that of Sir William Pepperrell.[3]

It is ironic that Baronet Pepperrell, the one true aristocrat and peer in the region of the Piscataqua, called Kittery his home, rather than the more elegant Portsmouth. But he was not born into the aristocracy; he earned his way into it. Throughout his life, he remained the simple son of a simple fisherman and the Maine town suited him well.

Years later, in 1799, the United States government would take several islands in the middle of the river and create the Portsmouth Naval Shipyard on them. It would become a ship-building and repair facility for the United States Navy that is still in existence. During the Second World War, Portsmouth became a dedicated construction facility for submarines.

That work continued during the Cold War years when Portsmouth produced both attack and ballistic missile submarines, including the Navy's second ballistic missile sub, the *U.S.S. Abraham Lincoln.*

For years, the states of Maine and New Hampshire argued over which entity had legal jurisdiction over the shipyard, mainly because of its island location. Finally, in 1993, the United States Supreme Court ruled that Seavey Island is totally within the boundaries of the State of Maine. The legal ruling hasn't changed the way local residents refer to the "Navy yard." New Hampshire residents call it the "Portsmouth" yard; Maine residents call it the "Kittery" yard.

---

[3] Roberts, Kenneth, *Northwest Passage*, p. 295.

"To The Uttermost Of My Power"

ONCE MARRIED AND SETTLED ON PROPERTY BORDERING HIS FATHER-IN-LAW'S, Colonel William Pepperrell embarked on two major undertakings. One was creating a family to carry on the name and the family traditions. The second was to build and expand his already fast-moving business. He was successful in both activities.

Family-wise, Colonel Pepperrell and Margery had a total of seven children, all of who survived to adulthood, an extreme rarity in those days.

The children arrived as follows:

- Andrew, born July 1, 1680 -- the original heir apparent to the Pepperrell business;
- Mary, born September 5, 1685 -- she married three times and had a total of 16 children;
- Margery, born 1689 -- her second husband was a judge in the Court of Appeals in Kittery;
- Joanna, born June 22 1692 -- she married a local physician;
- Miriam, born September 5, 1694 -- she married a prominent Boston merchant;
- William, June 27, 1696 -- the future baronet;
- Dorothy, born July 28, 1698 -- she married one of the captains working in the Pepperrell fleet;
- Jane, born in 1701 -- she married twice, each time to prominent members of the Maine and New Hampshire communities.

As the family grew, so did the family business, now called "William Pepperrell and Son." Each year, more

"To The Uttermost Of My Power"

and more Pepperrell ships made more and more voyages to more and more ports on both sides of the Atlantic. Pepperrell cargo holds now carried many more new and exciting products and goods to tantalize and intrigue buyers back home in the Kittery-Portsmouth area. All the while, Colonel Pepperrell continued to make plans for his first-born son Andrew to join the venture.

Life was looking good for the young emigrant, his family and his business.

"To The Uttermost Of My Power"

Chapter III

The Pepperrell Enterprise

COLONEL WILLIAM PEPPERRELL WAS NOT AN EDUCATED MAN. HE WAS A SMART, ENTERPRISING, AMBITIOUS INDIVIDUAL WHO WANTED TO GET AHEAD; HE JUST NEVER HAD THE OPPORTUNITY OR THE TIME FOR VERY MUCH FORMAL SCHOOLING.

Apprenticed to a fishing captain at an early age, he learned his lessons on the high seas and on the fishing banks off Newfoundland. He knew how to sail a ship, and how to catch and cure fish. And he was eager to learn how to turn those skills into money.

Colonial Kittery was a good place to do it.

By the time Colonel William Pepperrell had married Margery Bray and moved to Kittery Point, he had already been shipping loads of fish north to Canada, south to the other colonies and east to Europe for sale in their hungry markets. When his partner, Ambrose Gibbons, left to go into business further down east in Maine, Pepperrell became the sole owner of the company. Now, he knew, it was time to expand it.

What he needed was cargo, ships and markets. The basic cargo at the start was simple and plentiful -- fish and lumber. The shipyards along the Piscataqua and the many men who braved the sea to fish provided the product to fill the cargo holds. Within a few years, Pepperrell and Son managed seven ships, the same number as Boston merchant Andrew Faneuil -- of Faneuil Hall fame. Soon the Kittery firm would compete

"TO THE UTTERMOST OF MY POWER"

with other, better-known Boston traders such as the one eventually run by John Hancock.

The markets were plentiful as well. Initially, the Colonel found the trade with Newfoundland and other Canadian settlements to be profitable, and he also began dealing with a variety of accessible ports in Europe. Then his ships turned south to other colonial ports such as Boston, Providence, New Haven, New York, Philadelphia, Baltimore, Wilmington and other ports in North Carolina, and Charleston. The trading company also ventured across the Atlantic to the Azores, the Canary Islands and some of the other African ports.

Most of the trading voyages undertaken by the Colonel involved the classic triangular route designed to handle the variety of trade and to maximize profits. For example, his ship might leave Kittery loaded with fish and timber and head for New York. There the fish and timber would be sold and the captain would purchase hard good items, such as nails and other tools and a variety of building items. The ship then might sail to the Caribbean to sell the tools at a profit, and buy a new cargo consisting of sugar, molasses and dried tropical fruit, which would have a good market in Maine.

In some cases, a Pepperrell trading voyage might conclude at the second or third stop with the sale, not only of the cargo, but the ship as well. Then the profit from this sale would be reinvested in the business by the purchase of a new ship built at one of the Kittery shipyards.

A good example of an early Pepperrell trading venture is that of the bark *Mary* in 1696. Leaving Kittery, she carried in her hold a variety of items, including 11,500 red oak hogshead staves, 9,975 feet of pine boards,

"To The Uttermost Of My Power"

8,350 shingles, nearly 14,000 pounds of cod and haddock, and eight barrels of mackerel.[4]

Pepperrell's agents in Barbados sold the cargo for 136 pounds English money, and then reloaded the ship with Caribbean molasses and sugar and other items worth 339 pounds that would be sold to eager customers in the Kittery-Portsmouth area.

Although the French and British colonies were not allowed to trade with each other legally, local officials were inclined to look the other way as a lucrative trade developed during the peacetime years. Smuggling was, in many ways, considered a quasi-honorable and profitable profession, and there is little doubt that the Colonel on occasion carried contraband cargo in some of his ships.

Trading with the French could be dangerous and tragic, however. In the summer of 1723, the Colonel learned that either French or Indian traders at Canso on Cape Breton Island killed Captain John Watkins, his own son-in-law. Profits often had a price.

A NUMBER OF PEPPERRELL SHIPS APPARENTLY TRADED WITH PORTS ALONG THE WEST COAST OF AFRICA, also known at that time as the Slave Coast. There is no evidence, however, the Pepperrells ever took part in the infamous "middle passage" that brought hundreds of thousands of Black slaves across the Atlantic.

In 1719, however, the Pepperrell agent in Barbados sent them a cargo that included a shipment of rum and five slaves. The rum apparently sold well, but the human

---

[4] Rolde, Neil, Sir William Pepperrell of Colonial New England, p. 6-7.

"To The Uttermost Of My Power"

cargo was more fragile. Four of the slaves arrived in Kittery dead, and the fifth died shortly thereafter. Their fate helped to convince the Pepperrells that the slave trade probably would not be profitable in New England

The family did own slaves, however. Records indicate the Pepperrells may have at one time owned as many as a dozen slaves who handled a variety of jobs and chores at what was now called the Pepperrell Mansion, or at one of the family business operations. In those days, slave owning was legal and acceptable even in New England, and it was quite common for leading families such as the Pepperrells to own slaves to handle common household duties.

Nothing indicates the Pepperrells were harsh to their slaves. In fact, the Colonel freed his mulatto body slave in his will and arranged for another to receive manumission when he reached age 40. The second generation at the helm of the family also owned slaves. At the very beginning of his own will, the younger William left to his widow "the use of any four of my slaves,"[5] implying he certainly owned others.

The major event of the era that impacted the trading business in the colonies, however, was war. When King William's War broke out, in 1689, the Pepperrell firm had to sail on disputed seas for nearly eight years of war with the French to reach the lucrative colonial markets to the north. French naval vessels and privateers prowled the

---

[5] William Pepperrell, Will, 11 January, 1759, Miscellaneous Manuscripts, Massachusetts Historical Society.

"To The Uttermost Of My Power"

sea-lanes between the English colonies, Newfoundland and Labrador, looking to capture any ship flying the Union Jack of Great Britain.

During this period, the Colonel did not curtail trade; rather he increased it in the other direction. His fleet of ships grew to nearly 20; the fleet included ships of varying sizes to account for distance and types of cargoes. Rather than head north into danger, the Colonel sent more and more of his trading voyages south to other English colonies. The Pepperrell firm built up a strong and thriving business with communities in North Carolina during the war years; that trade continued for decades after peace was finally achieved in King William's War.

Even as the business grew and more and more ships were added to the Pepperrell fleet, the family still did not sail their own vessels. Just as William did when he worked at the Isles of Shoals, the family either hired captains to sail the ships or let others do it for shares of the profits. The Pepperrells were fleet managers, route planners and agent correspondents who made the logistical details that others carried out. It was a very profitable arrangement.

That the trading business was growing was evidenced by the expansion of the Pepperrell homestead on the shore at Kittery Point. Fifteen-foot additions were added to each end of the home to provide additional rooms for the growing family. The Pepperrells also attended more diligently to the landscaping and grounds of what was rapidly becoming an estate.

The Colonel was not just in the trading business. Landless when he left England, the patriarch saw the great expanses of land available in America, and he

"To The Uttermost Of My Power"

determined to acquire his share. Beginning with the acre given him by John Bray, the Colonel quietly acquired parcels of land stretching north along the coast of Maine. It was said during the years before the American Revolution that an individual could travel from Kittery to Saco -- more than 30 miles -- without leaving Pepperrell land.

William Pepperrell was making plans to involve his oldest son, Andrew, in the family business, expecting him to take over the lion's share of managing it while the father took more of an interest in the civic affairs of Kittery.

For many years, the Colonel was a selectman for the town, and for nine consecutive years he performed the crucial job of moderator at the community's annual town meeting. Although he had no legal training, the Colonel served as a justice of the peace and as a judge on the York County Court of Appeals. Later in life, he also served two terms as Kittery's representative to the Massachusetts General Court -- the colonial legislature -- in Boston.

Both the Colonel and his father-in-law and fellow Devonshire native, John Bray, were Anglicans when they arrived in America. But the Puritans had long ruled in Boston where religion was concerned. The Massachusetts Bay Colony never included religious tolerance as one of its founding principles and Anglicans could neither live nor worship within its borders.

Things were different 70 miles north in Maine, which had no Puritan tradition. Maine and nearby New Hampshire had a history of relative religious tolerance. Leading men and families from both sides of the river attended St. John's Church, the Anglican edifice in Portsmouth.

"To The Uttermost Of My Power"

Bray and Pepperrell, however, would worship on the Maine side of the Piscataqua. They both became founding members of Kittery Point's Congregational Church, which began holding services in 1714 under Rev. John Newmarch. That church in Kittery Point -- the First Congregational Church -- today is the oldest sanctuary in Maine. The building there dates from 1730; several fires over the years destroyed the first structure.

As the 17th century came to a close, Kittery had experienced problems that made the citizens much more aware of the French colony to the north and the savagery of its Indian allies. During King Phillip's War, some 60 residents were killed during an Indian raid. Several local communities -- Salmon Falls, New Hampshire and Wells, Maine, were attacked and local citizens slaughtered, and many homes and public buildings set on fire. York to the north was nearly destroyed. In 1690, Kittery again was raided, with substantial loss of life.

As noted before, Bray and Pepperrell had become active in the local frontier militia, with father and sons serving as officers in the York County volunteers. One account written by an unknown soldier talks about famed Indian fighter Col. Benjamin Church leading his detachment to "Pepperrell's fort", no doubt a reference to a private stockade somewhere on the property. The Colonel was also charged with overseeing the construction -- on orders from Boston -- of Fort William, a gun battery that formed the first defensive position to protect the Piscataqua region from attack by sea.

The exact location of Fort William is unknown today, but it is likely it eventually became the site of Fort McClary, a defensive blockhouse and battery site on the Kittery Point shoreline overlooking Pepperrell Cove that dates

"To The Uttermost Of My Power"

from the War of 1812, and which was used for coastal defense until the Civil War.

Meanwhile, Pepperrell's plan for an orderly transition to the next generation in his business came to a tragic ending when his eldest son and heir apparent, Andrew, died in 1713 at the age of 32. His passing was an unexpected, devastating shock, as was so much death in those days. Andrew's passing certainly cast a pall over the family members, their friends and their customers.

William Jr. was 17 when his brother died and, while he had worked in the business, no one had planned on him being the one to take over management of William Pepperrell and Son.

But now that was his destiny.

"To The Uttermost Of My Power"

Chapter IV

Under New Management

ANDREW PEPPERRELL WAS BURIED IN THE FAMILY CEMETERY AT KITTERY POINT BY HIS GRIEVING MOTHER, FATHER, SISTERS, BROTHER AND HIS FAMILY.

His parents made arrangements to support Andrew's widow -- the former Jane Eliot from a prominent Portsmouth family -- and the two small daughters he left behind. Andrew had lived in Newcastle, on the south shore of the river, almost directly across from the Pepperrell Mansion.[6]

With his older brother dead and gone, 17-year-old William Pepperrell, Jr. prepared to take up the reins of commerce. Because he was not supposed to inherit the business, William's early education had been rudimentary at best. He learned to read, write and do basic calculations at early versions of the Kittery Point village school, which didn't become a permanent town feature until 1707. He also had a private tutor for lessons in sailing and navigation.

Pepperrell apparently had very good penmanship, which his father recognized and put to good use. By age 12, he was working in his father's counting house and, by age 16, he was the clerk of the local court.

Then Andrew died.

---

[6] Jane Pepperrell remarried a few years later. She and Charles Frost had several children of their own. Jane Eliot Pepperrell Frost died in 1749.

"To The Uttermost Of My Power"

Due to his own energy, his father's age -- the Colonel was 67 -- and the pressure on his father's time due to outside interests, William Pepperrell, Jr. began to quickly take control of the family business.

One of the first things he and his father did was to change the name from "William Pepperrell and Son" to "Messers. William Pepperrell," telling customers far and wide that the company had changed, and it was now run by two very different William Pepperrells.

Byron Fairchild, in his 1954 study of the family business, noted that in the colonial era, there were basically two kinds of merchants. The first variety -- called the merchant/shopkeeper -- normally began his business life as a shopkeeper selling either specific craft goods such as candlesticks, or a small variety of needed items. As the demand for goods grew, this class of merchant would begin to obtain more and more types of items, selling them in what often would be called a mercantile. They were the retailers of their day.

The second type of entrepreneur was the combination of merchant/shipbuilder, and the Pepperrells definitely belonged in this group. They were concerned not with the final distribution of goods, but rather used their fleets of ships to supply shopkeepers at either end of their routes with a steady stream of saleable and profitable items.[7] They were the wholesalers of their days.

As young William -- known now as "Captain" Pepperrell to distinguish him from the Colonel and to reflect his role as a captain of a cavalry unit in the local militia -- became more familiar with the business, his father went

---

[7] Fairchild, Byron, *The Messrs. William Pepperrell*, p. 37-38.

"To The Uttermost Of My Power"

ahead with his plan to focus more time on his community duties. Simultaneously, he paid closer attention to his land acquisition activities. As he spent more and more of his time in his counting house on the family estate, the younger son took over operations of the trading business. He was said to be a friendly, congenial young man, interested in employing the best talents of family and friends.

He moved to expand business, increasing the Pepperrell fleet and looking for new markets to enter. He hired several of his brothers-in-law to be captains for the family fleet, and he encouraged several of his sisters to manage projects for the company. He also followed his father's practice of buying land, indeed, within several years, the family owned 5,000 acres that one day became the city of Saco, Maine -- later to be the home of the Pepperrell Manufacturing Company in the 19th century.

IN ADDITION TO MANAGING THE FIRM, PEPPERRELL ALSO FOUND TIME TO TAKE A WIFE AND START HIS OWN FAMILY. On a trip to Boston, he met Mary Hirst, the daughter of the wealthy Boston merchant Grove Hirst and granddaughter of Judge Samuel Sewell, the famous diarist and the chief justice of the Massachusetts Supreme Court.

Although born a blue blood, Mary had been orphaned when she was just 13, and she spent much of her time going back and forth throughout New England to live with a variety of relatives. One of those Sewell relations was Rev. Samuel Moody, of York, the town just to the north of Kittery. It was at the Moody parsonage that young Pepperrell courted Mary Hirst and where they worked out the details of their nuptials.

"To The Uttermost Of My Power"

It appears that Pepperrell had competition for her affections from her own cousin, Joseph Moody of York. Young Moody was a local schoolteacher with a fine reputation, but he couldn't compete with the wealthy young Mr. Pepperrell, who apparently used judicious purchases to solidify his hold on young Mistress Hirst's heart.

After a lengthy and apparently enjoyable courtship, the couple wed on February 23, 1723, in Boston, with the cream of the colony's business aristocracy in attendance. Her grandfather, Judge Sewall, conducted the ceremony. At the conclusion of more than a week of wedding festivities, the new couple left Boston on March 4, their destination Kittery.

What Mary found there was a home increasingly called the Pepperrell Mansion by the local residents. The two 15-foot additions to the original structure had added elegance to the home, not to mention the space needed to house the elder Pepperrell's family and the staff of servants and slaves required to manage the family. It was expected the brood would soon be growing as William and Mary began producing their children and heirs.

The house now boasted a gambrel roof that softened the harsh peaked roof look common to many New England homes, and a wooden carved pineapple -- the sign of hospitality in the American colonies -- was prominently featured on the front door. The property itself -- which included the elder Pepperrell's counting house -- was properly manicured and new features were added, including a fruit orchard and a deer park. The mansion would become Mary's home for the next 36 years of her life.

"To The Uttermost Of My Power"

Through the years, the mansion became a cultural and entertainment showplace for Kittery and the entire region, containing up to 50 full-length professional portraits of family members and what was probably the largest private library north of Boston.

CHILDREN APPEARED SLOWLY FOR THE YOUNGER PEPPERRELLS. On December 29, 1723, a daughter Elizabeth was born. She was followed by a son, Andrew -- named to honor Pepperrell's late brother and his great grandfather -- who was born January 4, 1726. Two subsequent children named William and Margery both died in infancy.

Compared to most colonial families, that of Captain William Pepperrell was very small. Even Queen Anne of Great Britain experienced 17 pregnancies during her life -- Mary Pepperrell had four. Based on average family size, the fact that only two of her four children survived to adulthood and her later history of illness, it is logical to assume that extensive childbearing was extremely difficult or perhaps even impossible for Mary Pepperrell.

The Pepperrells were strong believers in learning and they made sure the children received a quality education for those times, perhaps in reaction to the primitive schooling he had been subjected to as a boy. Their daughter Elizabeth, known as Betsy, attended the best schools in Boston, just as her mother had when she was young. Andrew, the pride and joy of the Pepperrells, did the same. Indeed, the Pepperrells spent a great deal of time in Boston; with Mary visiting the children while William handled his legislative duties.

Andrew joined the young elite of New England society when he entered Harvard College in Cambridge, Mass., at age 15 in 1741. Founded in 1650, Harvard was the

"To The Uttermost Of My Power"

first college established in the colonies and served during its early days as the training ground for New England's "fire and brimstone" clergymen. Andrew was not a divinity student. He graduated second in his class in 1744, with both a bachelor's and a master's degree.

It is interesting to look back and try and visualize the relationship between the two William Pepperrells nearly three centuries ago. It obviously was a good working relationship as William, the future baronet, followed in the proverbial footsteps of William, the Colonel. Not only did William Jr. take over and enhance the business his father had started, he actively took over many of the older man's civic duties, as the Colonel grew older. The father was a judge, the son was a chief judge; the father belonged to the General Court in Boston; so did the son, who also was a Governor's Councilor for 32 years. The father led the local militia; so did the son; but he also commanded the New England Land Forces in 1745. William the Baronet seemed to enhance the success of the family on the path his father originally took.

In addition, when the future baronet married, he and his bride moved into the family mansion with his parents. He certainly had the money to build his own home in the vicinity like his son Andrew eventually did, but he and Mary remained in the home he would inherit at the Colonel's death. When the Baronet died, his wife built her own home close to, but separate from, the mansion.

William and Mary didn't spend all their time with the elder Pepperrells, of course. The couple and their children spent a great deal of time in Boston, when there they lived in the Pepperrell house on Summer Street.

"TO THE UTTERMOST OF MY POWER"

All told, it does appear that father and son did have a good relationship, something that certainly helped promote the teamwork needed to run such an operation.

Business-wise, the firm moved along well and prospered under the younger William Pepperrell's leadership for the first decade and more. Then, in 1734, Colonel William Pepperrell died at the age of 87.

SINCE THE DEATH OF ANDREW, THE LIFE OF THE PEPPERRELL PATRIARCH IN KITTERY HAD SLOWED DOWN CONSIDERABLY, and his passing was quiet and peaceful. His widow, Margery, outlived him by seven years, passing away in 1741 at age 81.

In his will, the Colonel freed his mulatto body slave, left small bequests to his children, set aside money to buy a silver communion set for the Congregational Church in Kittery Point, provided a small stipend for the Rev. John Newmarch, and left money to help feed the poor and hungry in Kittery and for those back at his original home in Tavistock, Devonshire, England.

He left the company and the bulk of his estate to his surviving son, William, who was 38 years old. William now took possession of the Pepperrell Mansion as his own. He also inherited a house in Portsmouth and one in Boston.

The passing of the Colonel warranted an obituary notice in the Boston News-Letter, which normally only noted the deaths of prominent political leaders. His son also received a letter from Governor Jonathan Belcher offering his condolences and noting, "After Abraham

"To The Uttermost Of My Power"

died, God Blessed Isaac. May you, sir, go forth and prosper."[8]

And prosper Pepperrell did as he sought ways to expand his business over the years. The family's fleet of ships continued to grow, the count at times varying from 35 to 100 depending on who one spoke to and at what time of the year. The vessels ranged in size from small fishing boats to a brigantine of nearly 100 tons and the square-rigged ship *Eagle* of more than 180 tons.

ONE OF PEPPERRELL'S FAVORITE SHIPS WAS THE BRIGANTINE *KITTERY*. During its run to prominence, the Pepperrell firm often favored the brigantine as the workhorse of their fleet. Brigantines are two-mast vessels, with one mast square-rigged and the second normally fore-and-aft boom rigged. These riggings are operated from a boom close to the deck, which requires fewer crewmembers than square-riggers, where men aloft handle the sails.

In addition to the brigantines, other Pepperrell vessels included snows, with two-square rigged masts; schooners, usually with two or more fore-and-aft rigged masts; and sloops, ships with a single mast fore-and-aft rigged.

Beginning in 1742, the swift *Kittery* carried Pepperrell cargoes to Europe, Africa and the Caribbean. In November 1751, a hurricane off Cadiz, Spain, drove the *Kittery* onto rocks outside the harbor where the ship and most of the crew were lost. [9]

As the fleet grew so did the black ink on the family ledger sheet. For example, entries for the period from April of

---

[8] Parsons, Usher, *The Life of Sir William Pepperrell*, p. 31.
[9] Fairchild, p. 138.

"To The Uttermost Of My Power"

1717 to March of 1719 indicate a total of retail sales of more than 3,000 items brought in revenues of 6,489 English pounds. By comparison, the entire tax evaluation for Portsmouth in 1719 was only 3,722 English pounds.

Pepperrell himself was actively involved in all aspects of the operations. He personally purchased all the boots his ship captains wore, one year buying as many as 29 pair. He selected and hired all the captains, and while he eagerly sought relatives for those posts, they had to be competent.

Pepperrell also personally supervised the construction of all family ships in local shipyards, making sure the vessels were well built and seaworthy. He was the one who selected cargoes to be transported and sold, and he also chose the routes taken and the markets entered.

Much of the firm's excess capital was kept in company bank accounts in London, allowed the Pepperrells to become involved in the lending industry, almost like bankers themselves. Good customers could draw money on their accounts, much like a checking account, payable back to the Pepperrells at a certain date. The company also made substantial loans to customers, the interest rates varying due to economic conditions. When Sir William died in 1759, he had more than 6,000 pounds on deposit in London.

Judicious investment of excess profits allowed William to buy additional parcels of land. One such purchase was for land that would eventually become the town of Scarborough. He also bought substantial plots of land in the Damariscotta region of Maine, where the Waldo family had major holdings.

"To The Uttermost Of My Power"

Always profitable, by the time of the Colonel's death in 1734, the Pepperrell firm was a thriving enterprise that could rival any other merchant trading company in Boston or in other cities along the east coast. They did it not by luck or innovation, but by consistency and dependability. They bought good ships, hired good captains and lost few cargoes. Customers could and would depend upon them to deliver what they promised. It was a reputation that William Pepperrell, Jr. would build upon while making his family one of the wealthiest in any of the thirteen colonies.

As time went by and his family grew older, William Pepperrell was able to get some help in managing his company from other family members. One came through marriage.

Pepperrell's daughter Betsy was said to be a happy and an attractive young woman, and she must have been "the marriage" catch of the colonies.

Eventually, she married a young man from Rhode Island named Nathaniel Sparhawk on May 1, 1742. The groom was the stepson of merchant Jonathan Waldo and the stepbrother of her father's great friend Samuel Waldo. Their new home, Sparhawk Hall, became yet another Kittery landmark and young Sparhawk began to lend a hand to his father-in-law with the family business. Sparhawk never gained any sort of control over the enterprise -- in fact he ran his own trading company, Sparhawk & Colman until it went bankrupt in 1758 -- and it seems that Pepperrell was reluctant to give him or anyone too much control of the family business.

Another potential assistant came to Pepperrell in the form of distant relative Charles Chauncey. He too

"TO THE UTTERMOST OF MY POWER"

provided help to Pepperrell but never to the extent that was expected of his son and heir, Andrew.

At the time of his father's passing, William seemed to take a more serious look at religion. He became more involved with the Kittery Point Congregational Church, as his father had. He became a friend of Rev. John Newmarch, and a special friend of a new minister who, beginning in 1751, shared the pulpit with Rev. Newmarch for several years. Rev. Benjamin Stevens would provide constant comfort when family tragedies occurred later in Pepperrell's life. Pepperrell also became involved in the administration of the church and often represented Revs. Newmarch and/or Stevens at meetings with other churches through the region. He often represented the entire congregation at a variety of ecclesiastical events including the ordination of new ministers at various churches.

His written correspondences -- which were voluminous and included a large number of recipients throughout the colonies -- changed as well. He now included more references to God in his letters and began to attribute the outcome of more and more things in his daily life to the direct intervention of the Almighty. He certainly was not alone in these kinds of public attributions to divine goodwill.

Just after his father's death, Pepperrell responded to the condolences sent to him by his life-long friend, Samuel Waldo. He wrote: "I take kindly your expression of sorrow for my great loss in the death of my aged and honored father, and desire that God in his great goodness and mercy would be pleased to fit and prepare

"To The Uttermost Of My Power"

us all for that untried state of existence to which we are all hastening."[10]

Throughout the remaining years of his life, Pepperrell hosted and befriended a large number of theologians and ministers, many of whom were frequent guests in his home.

IN THE COLONIAL DAYS OF WILLIAM PEPPERRELL, money was one barometer of success, but the ultimate marker of respectability was, just as in England, land. And the Pepperrells had, thanks to both Williams' purchasing, an abundance of land. In fact before long, most of the undeveloped land on either side of the Piscataqua River was Pepperrell land.

THE PEPPERRELLS WERE EARLY ON CONSIDERED TO BE ONE OF THE MORE RESPECTABLE FAMILIES IN KITTERY, and worthy of consideration for a role in the town government. The Colonel served as a selectman for several terms, was the town meeting moderator for nine consecutive years, and served on the commissions that ultimately created the towns of South Berwick, Berwick, North Berwick and Eliot when these towns were separated from Kittery. He also served as a judge of the local court and represented the town in Boston's colonial legislature for two terms.

Upon his passing, the town needed to replace him in several offices and officials soon found out that the son had a hunger and an aptitude for public service in Kittery as well as in the provincial capital at Boston.

During this era, nine families seemed to run Kittery, and they took turns holding key local offices. They were the

---

[10] Parsons, Pepperrell to Waldo, p. 29.

"To The Uttermost Of My Power"

Pepperrell, the Cutts and the Gunnison families from Kittery Point, and the Frost, Shapleigh, Dennett, Hammond, Emery and Leighton clans from Kittery proper.

In 1720 at the age of 24 and well before the death of his father, Captain Pepperrell was asked to represent Kittery and its environs at the Massachusetts General Court -- the colonial representative assembly in Boston. His diligent good work in his first term earned him a second and then a third. He soon became a well-known and well-respected political figure in the more cosmopolitan atmosphere of Boston.

In 1727, he was chosen by Governor William Dummer to serve on the Massachusetts Governor's Council. This group of 35 citizens served as advisors to the colonial governor and, was in effect, the "upper house" of the legislature, functioning much like the Parliament's House of Lords. And, as an institution, it still exists today.

Pepperrell served on that body for the next 32 years, and, in doing so, he was able to chart his way through dangerous waters during the rule of five successive governors of colonial Massachusetts. For the last 18 of those years, he presided as head of the council and worked with the governors -- especially Governor William Shirley -- on a wide range of political matters that affected residents in greater Massachusetts as well as the District of Maine.

During those years, Pepperrell became an expert on military and Indian affairs and generally represented the council when investigations of frontier problems or situations took place anywhere in the colony and especially in the district of Maine.

"To The Uttermost Of My Power"

Pepperrell also took his father's place as judge on the York County Court -- which included Kittery -- in 1725. Five years later, he was elevated to chief justice by Governor Jonathan Belcher. Although he had no formal legal training, this was not considered a cause for disqualification. In fact, many people felt he had the right temperament for the job and that he was sophisticated enough to handle all types of people who might appear before him.

He was a realist, however, and a man who understood his shortcomings. Always willing to improve himself, he had some of his captains buy him a variety of books and commentaries on English law for his own study efforts to become a better-qualified jurist.

MOST OF THE CASES THAT CAME BEFORE JUSTICE PEPPERRELL, while he sat on the bench, were simple, easily handled matters, mainly dealing with common law marriage issues. One case, however, that came into his court in 1734 -- Frost v. Leighton -- became a landmark decision in several areas on the appellate level.

According to tradition, the Crown had the right of ownership to any tree in North America that could be used as a ship's mast. In 1734, Sir Ralph Gulston, on behalf of the Admiralty, commissioned Samuel Waldo to obtain a number of masts for a series of new ships planned for construction. Waldo, in turn, hired William Leighton of Kittery to do the work. Leighton eventually found a stand of trees on property known as the Caroline Farm in the Berwick section of Kittery. John Frost of Kittery was the property owner. According to court papers, Leighton cut down seven trees and trimmed and removed six, each one three feet in diameter.

"To The Uttermost Of My Power"

For some time prior to this, however, landowners in the district of Maine had begun to resent this royal prerogative of taking any tree the government wanted and at no cost. Frost was one of them.

He promptly filed suit charging trespass and loss of property against Leighton and sought monetary damages of 200 pounds. The case was heard in April at the Court of Common Pleas in York, Maine, Chief Justice Pepperrell presiding.

Leighton's defense attorney was a lawyer from Boston named William Shirley. Shirley pled his case, but the court found in favor of Frost and ordered immediate payment. Shirley quickly appealed the ruling to Superior Court in Boston. That court, however, upheld the original ruling and ordered that damages be paid.

This was one of the first legal challenges to the King's authority on a variety of issues that impacted American life, much like the Stamp Act in the 1760s. As a judge, Pepperrell kept that challenge alive.

Over the next few years, Frost v. Leighton made its way slowly through a variety of courts and councils both in North America and in England. Leighton got a new lawyer, William Bollan, who appealed to Governor Jonathan Belcher and his council. But Belcher understood the unrest in Maine about the tree and mast issue, and he wanted to avoid stirring it up with another public trial. So he sent the case to England. Eventually, Leighton obtained two orders from the King and his Privy Council in London to have the ruling overturned. When these orders were presented to the Massachusetts superior and supreme courts, the judges were not impressed. They ruled that the colony's royal charter contained no such procedure for the monarch to overrule

"To The Uttermost Of My Power"

the colonial courts and they confirmed the verdict for Frost.

Yet another blow was struck against tyranny.

BEYOND THE JUDICIARY, PEPPERRELL ALSO BECAME THE COLONEL OF THE YORK COUNTY MILITIA, WHICH WAS responsible for the defense of settlements from the Piscataqua region to the border of Canada. In reality, this was an immense responsibility. Not only was he charged with protecting the greater Kittery area, but also all the settlements along the rocky coast of Maine, and those at least as far inland as Fort Western, the modern day city and state capital of Augusta. Beyond the Fort Western area, there were few settlements and mostly vast woodlands. However, Pepperrell still had to safeguard those living in Maine from attack parties emerging from the forests. It was a huge job.

And, as an adjunct to his militia function, Pepperrell became well versed in dealing with the family of Abenaki Indian tribes living in Maine and other locations in New England. In July of 1727, just a month after he joined the governor's council, he and Lt. Gov. William Dummer attended a conference with more than 100 Indians and tribes to discuss a peace arrangement. The meeting was held at Falmouth, the site of present day Portland, Maine, and other officials, such as New Hampshire Lieutenant Governor John Wentworth, were in attendance. After that, whenever Massachusetts met with any Indian tribes at any place, Pepperrell usually was there.

By the mid-1730s, William Pepperrell was a most substantial man. He had inherited and expanded his father's business to where he was one of the wealthiest men in the colonies. He was an advisor to the governor

"To The Uttermost Of My Power"

of Massachusetts and was becoming more and more involved in colonial politics. He was a local judge, in fact the chief judge. He had married well and was waiting for his son to be old enough to help him with the business. Life was busy and prosperous for William Pepperrell.

His future seemed limitless.

"To The Uttermost Of My Power"

Chapter V

The Frontier On Fire

THROUGHOUT WILLIAM PEPPERRELL'S LIFE, ONE THING OVERSHADOWED EVERY DAILY ACTIVITY THAT HE AND HIS FELLOW PROVINCIALS DID -- THE IMMINENT THREAT OF WAR.

They lived in constant fear of attack from the north by the French and their savage Indian allies. The settlers all knew that at any time of any day they could be attacked and ruthlessly slaughtered in the field or in the home by the French and Indian war parties that would disappear just as silently as they had arrived from the wilderness.

For the first 17 years of William Pepperrell's life, the English colonies in North America knew only three years of real peace with the colony of New France on the cold shores of the St. Lawrence River. Mortal conflict between New France and the British colonies was inevitable, as they both strove to dominate the continent.

As colonies, they were quite different.

NEW FRANCE, founded by Samuel de Champlain in 1608, attracted few permanent "habitants" from France to make up a stable population. Instead, New France was a haven for fur trappers, traders, and fortune seekers of various questionable types who came to the remote location looking for riches. Some of these people would settle in New France, but most yearned for their ancestral homes in Europe. Only the Jesuits seemed willing to remain in the frozen expanse of Canada, but

"To The Uttermost Of My Power"

their objective was to save the souls of the Indian tribes they served.

A handful of French adventurers, trappers and traders also settled the Mississippi River delta and founded the city of New Orleans, but thousands of miles and hundreds of Indian tribes separated them from their countrymen in Montreal and Quebec.

THE ENGLISH COLONIES ON THE ATLANTIC SEABOARD WERE MUCH more settled than New France. They were there to stay. Whether they were a crown colony like the New England settlements where the King appointed the governor; a proprietorship such as Maryland and Pennsylvania, where a single family like the Calverts and the Penns were in control; or a charter colony such as Connecticut and Rhode Island, which elected their own governors; they were similar in that they were settled by people who had left their past behind in England and who were planning for a new and better life on the other side of the Atlantic. Farmers tilled fields far away from the coastline; coastal cities served as reception points for immigrants willing to move inland to unsettled areas; frontier towns cropped up with regularity as the settlers built farms and displaced Indian tribes.

Because they were closer to New France than the others, the "New England" colonies were well aware of the dangers of those French and Indian war parties that could appear out of nowhere, brutally destroy a settlement and then disappear as quickly as they had come.

By 1745, each New England colony was very different. Massachusetts -- with its capital at Boston -- was the most populous colony, but its tradition of religious intolerance, derived from the Puritans, ruffled the

"To The Uttermost Of My Power"

feathers of some of the others. Maine was now part of the Massachusetts colony because of its sparse population and would remain so until 1820. Maine's neighbor, New Hampshire, had been ruled by a governor from Boston as late as 1741. Now that it had its own governor and its status as a colony restored, it was determined to retain its independence. Rhode Island had split from Massachusetts over religious freedom issues to become a haven of religious diversity, and its colonial government in Providence still deeply resented their northern neighbor. Connecticut had developed independently of the other colonies, but still warily guarded its own independence.

The other area that would eventually become a New England state, Vermont, was now contested land claimed by New Hampshire, New York and New France.

Both the British colonies and New France also coveted the huge Ohio River Valley just beyond the mountains, and it seemed to be ripe for the taking. The French wanted it for furs and natural resources; the British saw it as fertile farmland.[11]

When the French and British fought in Europe, they also fought in the New World. The British settlers were, for the most part, on the defensive, while the French and Indians attacked the English settlements and tried to wipe them off the face of the earth.

The first major colonial conflict was King Phillip's War, fought between settlers in southern New England and the local Indian tribes, the Wampanoags and the Mohegans. For two years -- 1675 and 1676 -- the frontier was ablaze with attacks and counterattacks.

---

[11] Eckert, Allen, *That Dark and Bloody River*, p. 1-14.

"TO THE UTTERMOST OF MY POWER"

The Wampanoag Chieftain Metacomet -- known to the colonists as King Phillip -- was finally defeated by the English settlers and peace returned to the region. But this bloody war set the tone for more to come.

KING PHILLIP'S WAR spread far enough to the north to affect Kittery. An Indian raid during that conflict left more than a dozen residents of the traditionally safe and established coastal town, dead and scalped in a gruesome lesson to always be alert.

This raid heightened the need for the settlers to unite for their own safety. Many men, including the Brays and the Pepperrells and other early residents of the region, quickly joined local militia organizations designed to protect their communities. In many towns, citizens built and maintained a community stockade, essentially a town fort made of four strong wooden walls, or "garrison houses" -- structures where the second story overhung the first to allow defenders to fire downward on would-be attackers. Most garrison houses also included narrow musket slits on the lower floor. It was hoped that these garrison houses would provide a refuge for people long enough to permit neighboring militias to mount a counterattack.

THE FIRST OF THE FRENCH AND INDIAN WARS TO IMPACT THE PISCATAQUA REGION WAS KING WILLIAM'S WAR (1689-1697), the American counterpart of the European War of the League of Augsburg. King William III had England join the League of Augsburg to prevent King Louis XIV from taking control of the Rhenish Palatinate -- an area near the Rhine River in today's Germany -- and increasing the power of France in Europe.

Under the command of New France's Governor-General, Louis de Buade, Count Frontenac, the French and their

"TO THE UTTERMOST OF MY POWER"

Indian allies brought war and terror to the northern colonies. The first community raided was Schenectady, New York; next they came closer, striking Salmon Falls and Durham, New Hampshire; and then raiding Falmouth (now Portland) and Wells, in Maine. Homes were burned, hundreds killed, and many more taken captive and led north to Canada where most of them were lost forever among the Indian tribes.

Kittery was struck in 1690, when a number of Pepperrell's friends were killed in a random attack. Two years later, the village of York, Maine, just to the north of Kittery, was raided by a French and Indian war party from Canada. The enemy column struck quickly before any alarms could be sounded or requests for help be sent to neighboring towns. Many settlers were killed and scalped where they were found. Dozens of survivors were roped together and started along the trail to the North. There in the French settlements, some would be left behind as slaves, some would be tortured and burned for entertainment, and the rest would be sent north to distant villages.

Meanwhile, the survivors in York buried their dead and rebuilt their homes, but this time on a safer, higher elevation.

THE FINAL COMMUNITY TARGETED WAS HAVERHILL, IN NORTHERN MASSACHUSETTS. This last raid also left posterity with a legend and a story that still chills the reader's heart today. It is the story of Hannah Dustin, a 40-year-old mother of nine who had recently given birth to a daughter. On the night of March 15, 1697, the Abenaki Indians and their French leaders attacked the unsuspecting settlement.

"TO THE UTTERMOST OF MY POWER"

The Indians took Hannah, her infant daughter Martha, and neighbor Mary Neff prisoners and started them on the long march to remote Indian villages in Canada. When Hannah couldn't stop baby Martha from crying, she was forced to watch an Indian crush Martha's head against a tree. The Indians took the women to an island in the Merrimac River near what today is the town of Boscawen, NH. Among other captive's there, Hannah met Benjamin Lennardson, a 14-year-old boy the Indians had captured in another raid.

Hannah, Mary and Benjamin decided they would try to escape before they were taken north and out of reach of their families or any would-be rescuers from the militia who might be on their trail.

That night Hannah was able to free bonds and then those of Mary and Benjamin without being heard. Then they stole the Indians' tomahawks while they slept. With those deadly weapons, they attacked and killed 10 of the 12 Indians -- allowing only a woman and a boy to escape their fury. The trio scalped the dead Indians and brought the grisly items with them for proof of what they had done.

Using Indian canoes and traveling only at night, they moved down the Merrimack for several days and finally reached Haverhill and safety. In the aftermath of their return, the Massachusetts General Court honored the three and also voted them financial awards of nearly 25 pounds each for killing the Indians.

Today, a statue stands in Haverhill, honoring Hannah, Mary and Benjamin in their effort to escape from Indian captivity.[12]

---

[12] Leckie, Robert, *A Few Acres of Snow*, p. 197-198.

"To The Uttermost Of My Power"

KING WILLIAM'S WAR ENDED SOON AFTER THE INDIAN RAID ON HAVERHILL AND HANNAH DUSTIN'S HEROISM. The 1697 Treaty of Ryswick ended the fighting the war and restored the status quo in the colonies. As such, the treaty solved little, either in Europe or North America, and it merely laid the foundation for the next conflict, which was sure to come.

It came in 1702.

In Europe, it was called the War of the Spanish Succession, and it was fought unsuccessfully to keep the French ruling family of Bourbon from gaining the throne of Spain. It spilled over into the colonies as Queen Anne's War and again pitted New France against the British settlements.

Once again the French and Indians attacked settlements along the frontier, burning farms and fields, killing men, women and children, and taking captives back to Canada.

The most brutal attack took place at Deerfield, Massachusetts in 1704. While settlers flocked to garrison houses and other fortified locations, unfortunate white prisoners were dragged off to Indian villages where they were adopted into tribes.[13]

Later in the war, British troops from Massachusetts were able to conquer the French colony of Acadia, which subsequently was known as Nova Scotia. It was returned to France when the warring alliances approved the Treaty of Utrecht in 1713 to end this conflict.

---

[13] Demos, John, *The Unredeemed Captive*, p. 1-50.

"To The Uttermost Of My Power"

After Queen Anne's War, an uneasy peace settled over North America. French trappers and traders spread out even further into the interior of the continent, and settlers from the British colonies moved out beyond the Appalachian Mountains. Both activities were a recipe for a future war.

EVEN THOUGH FRANCE AND GREAT BRITAIN WERE AT PEACE, SOMETIMES THE COLONIES WERE NOT. Into this category falls the tragic story of Father Rale.

Sebastien Rale was a Jesuit priest who came to New France in 1669, as part of the group that accompanied the new Governor-General, Count Frontenac, to Quebec. He spent several years working at missions founded with some of the Western tribes and in 1694, he was sent to minister to the Abenaki Indians who lived along the Kennebec River in Maine. By 1698, Father Rale had built his own church at Norridgewock, on the Kennebec.

Father Rale was a fine missionary and a good friend to the Indians, but he was also concerned about English settlers encroaching on lands that belonged to New France. He knew his Indians could certainly improve the situation.

Over the years, Indian raids and incursions on settlers in Maine seemed to steadily increase. That fact caused diametrically opposed portraits of Father Rale to come into play. In the New England colonies, he was thought to be a bloodthirsty Catholic priest/butcher inciting Indians at his mission to attack and massacre settlements across the border in Maine. French writers in Canada described him as a saintly man trying to lead his flock to paradise. There was no middle ground.

"To The Uttermost Of My Power"

Several Massachusetts governors believed Father Rale was inciting violence on the frontier. In 1710, the priest escaped from one attempt to capture him at Norridgewock that was launched by Governor William Dudley.

More than a decade later, in January of 1722, Governor Samuel Shute sent a force of 200 men to attack Norridgewock. They surrounded the settlement and moved in to complete their mission only to find that Father Rale had been forewarned and he had escaped deeper into Canada.

As revenge for this English attack, the French government sent a party of French and Indian troops against the town of Brunswick farther down on the Kennebec, and close to Merrymeeting Bay, where that river joins with the Androscoggin before emptying into the Atlantic Ocean. On June 13, 1723, they attacked the Maine community and left it ravished and in flames.

Farther south, Lieutenant Governor William Dummer had succeeded Governor Shute.[14] Dummer then launched what would be termed "Dummer's War," designed to end once and for all the Indian threat posed by Father Rale and the Norridgewock Indians.

In August 1724, Dummer ordered a militia force of 300 men to destroy Father Rale's mission. The armed group left Fort Richmond on the Kennebec River in a fleet of 17 whaleboats bound for the Norridgewock Abenaki mission, hoping to end the threat from Father Rale forever.

---

[14] In 1727, Governor Dummer invited a new member to join the Governor's Council -- William Pepperrell of Kittery, Maine.

"To The Uttermost Of My Power"

As they approached the village, the force divided into two groups led by Captains Jeremiah Moulton and Johnson Harmon. Each leader told his men that Father Rale was not to be harmed and should be captured alive.

In the morning of August 24, taking advantage of the element of surprise, the two columns rushed quickly into the still-sleeping village. Quickly the Indians and their French allies were roused and began to defend their settlement. At the forefront was Father Rale.

One account of the attack said the priest was found in a tent with a young English captive and several scalps that somehow were identified as being taken from victims of Indian raids on Maine settlements. Whatever the truth was, Father Rale fought so strenuously that he could not be taken alive. He was slain and scalped and his mutilated body was left behind when the English column left the village ablaze.

After suffering some light casualties and seeing that their mission was completed, Moulton and Harmon led their men quickly back toward Fort Richmond, the site of present-day Waterville, Maine. There was no pursuit.

Father Rale's mutilated body was reverently buried under the altar of his church; his scalp was redeemed for hard money in Boston.

Immediately after he was slain, Father Rale became an instant martyr to the French and continued to be portrayed as a monster by the English. He and his legacy were caught in the religious conflagration that was always a part of the French and Indian wars.

"To The Uttermost Of My Power"

Even today, Father Rale remains a controversial figure in colonial history. Today, the missionary is revered by the French, the Canadians, and the Catholics. Many in the English colonies and later in the United States remember him as the "black robe" who unleashed the savage Indian tribes on unsuspecting settler villages.

As in most things, the truth probably lies somewhere in between.

THE NEXT WAR BETWEEN THE FRENCH AND BRITISH WOULD NOT COME UNTIL 1744. The War of the Austrian Succession would be known as King George's War in North America, and it would provide a worldwide stage for William Pepperrell of Kittery Point.

He had been preparing for it for quite a while. He was well aware of the dangers facing all colonists as they attempted to create a new life for themselves so far away from England. Kittery and Kittery Point had suffered minor losses to the French and their Indian allies, but raids and attacks on York, Wells and other nearby communities certainly reminded Pepperrell of the dangers of living on the frontier.

Usher Parsons, Pepperrell's 19th century biographer, paints the picture of the young child cradled in his mother's arm and listening to her tell tales about atrocities committed by the Indians during their 1690 attack on Kittery. Margery Pepperrell told her son: "how her neighbor and intimate friend, Major Charles Frost -- was waylaid and shot while returning from church -- how her neighbor, Mr. Shapleigh, was killed, his son taken captive, his fingers bitten off and the bleeding vessels seared off with a hot iron -- how her Intimate friend, Mrs. Ursula Cutts, after spreading her hospitable

"To The Uttermost Of My Power"

board for the Waldron family, and awaiting their arrival for dinner, was pounced upon by lurking savages, and herself and field laborers tomahawked and killed -- how 21 persons were killed or taken captive at Sandy Beach (Rye), only three or four miles away."[15]

So Pepperrell literally grew up on the frontier war stories that circulated through the colonies. No wonder that at age 16, he was a member of the York County regiment of militia, which was responsible for defending the entire region from the Piscataqua River to the Canadian border. By the middle of the 1720s, William Pepperrell succeeded his father as colonel commanding the militia. Though France and England were seemingly at peace, alarms and incidents kept the eastern outposts in an almost constant state of readiness.

When war broke out in 1739 between England and Spain, Pepperrell summoned all his militia officers to a meeting to discuss problems of organization, discipline, and equipment. Vacancies in the volunteer ranks were filled, new companies were added to the regiment, and a new regiment was formed out of the militia from Falmouth eastward. Adopting a report of the council drafted by Pepperrell, the Massachusetts General Court voted funds to strengthen the harbor defenses of Boston, Salem, Marblehead, and the other coastal towns.

In the fall of 1743, when the situation became more threatening, Governor William Shirley notified Pepperrell that word of an imminent break with France had arrived from England. He directed Pepperrell "forthwith" to warn the exposed settlements against any sudden assault.

---

[15] Parsons, p. 21.

"To The Uttermost Of My Power"

The Maine militia, thanks to Pepperrell was ready. Settlements strengthened local stockades, drilled militia and upgraded their warning systems. Neighboring towns pledged to support and defend each other. Powder was stockpiled and new musket balls were made.

New England was on the defensive.

AS WE LOOK BACK IN TIME, even the War of the Revolution is so shrouded in the mists of history that it seems to be but myth and legend. In their own turn, the French and Indian Wars go back so far they can be construed as something akin to fairy tales. But make no mistake, these conflicts were full-fledged wars, full of death and destruction, blood and courage, religious hatred and betrayal, and merciless racial struggles of near annihilation. They were wars that displayed the very worst attributes of European society in the 17th and 18th century.

Seen primarily as sideshows for European wars, these North American conflicts were as serious as any struggle fought back on "the continent." The impact of their results multiplied again and again as the thirteen colonies matured into the United States and the new country grew into a true world power.

They were ethnic wars for the French and the English, natural and traditional enemies going back to the Norman Conquest of 1066.

They were religious wars fought between the Catholic French and the Protestant British. Each side thought God was an enlisted man in their army; each side was convinced the other would burn in Hell.

"To The Uttermost Of My Power"

And eventually they were racial wars involving those who had the most to lose, the American Indian tribes who were at a loss to deal with the Europeans. The French were their friends and treated them best; the English would use them and then ignore them if they had brought no value to the table.

Their true enemy, however, would prove to be the Americans, the Long Knives, whose farms and settlements were beginning to move further west and who would stop at nothing to acquire more Indian land. That war would go on for decades.

War drums were beating in 1744.

"To The Uttermost Of My Power"

Chapter VI

Louisbourg

A REVOLUTION HAD TAKEN PLACE IN LATE 17TH CENTURY FRANCE. IT WAS NOT A POLITICAL ONE, BUT A MILITARY REVOLUTION; A REVOLUTION IN STRATEGY, A REVOLUTION IN MILITARY ENGINEERING; A REVOLUTION THAT THE FRENCH WOULD BRING TO THE NEW WORLD.

France at that time was a tired country, worn out by the series of wars instigated and led by "the Sun King," Louis XIV. The nation's armies were weakened by the constant fighting during his long reign and morale in the surviving regiments was very low. Louis and his marshals were not even sure that France could defend her own borders, not to mention undertake offensive action. As alliance after alliance formed against the French, the situation seemed even more dire and threatening.

Someone had to do something to protect the Kingdom and it had to be done soon, before it was too late. The "someone" who did something was the Marquis de Vauban, a Marshal of France. What he did was design a new, stronger, nearly invincible system of fortifications. Vauban would prove to be the outstanding military genius of his era, and his ideas and tactics would be used into the 20th century.

Sebastien De Leprestre, Seigneur de Vauban and later Marquis de Vauban, was the foremost military strategist of his age, famed for his skill in both designing

"To The Uttermost Of My Power"

fortifications and in breaking through them. He also advised Louis XIV on how to consolidate France's borders, to make them more defensible. Vauban made a radical suggestion of giving up some land that was indefensible to allow for a stronger, less porous border with France's neighbors.

By the end of the 17th century, Vauban-designed fortresses were doing their job to protect the boundaries of France. Vauban's system of star-shaped forts with extending bastions, demi-lunes and sloping walls and gun emplacements, designed to provide overlapping fields of fire, had proven to be extremely versatile in defending difficult positions.

In British North America, concerned officials looked on as Vauban's ideas and technology gained a foothold on the continent after the Treaty of Utrecht that ended the War of the Spanish Succession and Queen Anne's War.

Under the terms of the treaty, France lost two possessions on the Canadian coast -- Acadia and Newfoundland. The French then decided to build a strong, Vauban-inspired fort on the shore of Cape Breton Island at a place ironically called English Harbor. The French would rename it Louisbourg. Construction there began in 1720, and it wasn't totally completed until 1744, just in time for war.

It was a costly venture. The building of Louisbourg helped to drain the French treasury. Louis XIV allegedly said that after spending so much money on the Atlantic fortifications, he should be able to see the spires of Louisbourg from his palace at Versailles.

"To The Uttermost Of My Power"

Over the years, Louisbourg gradually took shape. Without a doubt, it was the most traditional and European of the great forts the French built in North America. The flat and wind-swept ground leading to the sea was perfect for a Vauban facility, with its bastions, demi-lunes, revelines, redans, glacis and other defensive constructions taken right from Vauban's manuals. It was said some of the stone used to build the fortress was brought across the Atlantic from Rochefort, France.

Other fortresses built by French engineers in North America include those nearly invincible ones at Quebec and at Montreal, and two great stone forts on Lake Champlain -- Fort St. Frederic at Crown Point, and Fort Carillon, later named Ft. Ticonderoga by the conquering British.

The Atlantic fortifications were designed to blend in with the safe, natural harbor at Louisbourg, enclosing the facility on three sides by a thick, sloped wall in the best traditions of a Vauban fortress. In 1720, construction began on the King's Bastion, the largest gun battery within the town. Designed to be the town's "citadel," the King's Bastion was the largest building in North America at the time, and it was the military headquarters of the fortress. Also in that bastion were the governor's residence, the troop barracks, and the St. Louis Chapel, which served as the community's main church. The French finished this part of the fortress in 1729[16].

In 1731, the French began work on the Queen's Bastion, followed shortly thereafter by the Princess Bastion. Both of them provided heavy firepower to protect key parts of

---

[16] Wood, William, *The Great Fortress: A Chronicle of Louisbourg*, p. 1-14.

"To The Uttermost Of My Power"

the city walls. By the mid-1730s work was also progressing on the Brouillan, Maurepas and Place De La Grave bastions. The later bastion also featured a wall facing the harbor that would be lined with heavy artillery.

Key features of the fortress were two batteries designed to provide crushing artillery fire for the French defenders. The most imposing and dangerous was the 42-gun Royal or Grand Battery built at the far end of the harbor and designed to coordinate fire with the Dauphin Demi-bastion. Work on this position began in 1724 and it was completed in 1732.

The final defensive facility was the Island Battery, a dug-in position for a large number of 24-pound cannon, that, when combined with fire from the main fortress, was expected to destroy any enemy ship trying to enter the harbor of Louisbourg.

A major feature of the work included a full naval base that could serve as a homeport for the North American squadron of the French fleet. The naval base would also play a double role by serving as a repair and reconstruction facility for any and all kinds of French ships in the area. It would be a welcome stopping point for ships coming home to France after long globe-trotting missions in service to the Bourbons, as well as providing a final bit of France for ships before undertaking long global voyages.

By the 1740s, more than 4,000 residents lived at Louisbourg, and it was the fourth busiest port in North America, trailing only the British colonial cities of Boston, New York and Philadelphia. In 1743, the wall surrounding the city and linking the defensive bastions

"To The Uttermost Of My Power"

was completed. It was an awe-inspiring, frightening site to behold glowering over the sea routes to and from Europe. Louisbourg could and would threaten the lucrative fishing banks off the shore of Newfoundland. It certainly deserved the nicknames of the "Gibraltar of the Atlantic" and "the Dunkirk of North America."

LOUISBOURG NOW WAS INDEED A THRIVING COMMUNITY, and it had "only" cost 33 million livres (an incredible amount of money at that time) to build it. Fishing ships brought their catches to the port, ships leaving France stopped there after making the Atlantic crossing, and vessels heading for France could tarry there a few days before making the same crossing.

Ships carrying British flags also made frequent appearances at Louisbourg. Both England and France had outlawed trading between colonies, but policies made in London and Versailles were frequently ignored. This law was one of them and smuggling became one of the region's thriving industries.

No one knows how many of those English-flagged ships visiting Louisbourg carried the personal colors of William Pepperrell. But some of his captains surely made their way into the French fortress to trade goods and increase their profits.

The English Provincials were, of course, frightened to death of Louisbourg. Not only did it protect French possessions, but it provided a direct threat to the British fishing industry off Newfoundland, and it was in position to disrupt the commercial shipping that linked Boston with England and with points to the south of Massachusetts.

"To The Uttermost Of My Power"

Although the colonial officials and representatives of the commercial interests protested to London, nothing could be done because the two nations were technically at peace. In Portsmouth, Boston, Providence and Hartford, voices cried out for the destruction of the fortress. Even cities further south like New York and Philadelphia protested loudly but Louisbourg remained, a dagger aimed at the heart of New England.

Louisbourg, however, had its own weaknesses that reflected the weaknesses of New France. It had to do with the type of government the French settlements developed and how that government related to the people it ruled. It was the difference -- beyond language and religion -- between New England and New France.

For example, in Massachusetts much of the power was concentrated in the office of the Governor, the Governor's Council and the General Court. They controlled -- in conjunction with local officials -- the colonial militia, what might be called a colonial Navy, and generally the funding to carry out military plans and projects. If help were needed from Great Britain, the governor would ask for it. And as in previous cases, the governor would serve as a military leader.

New France, on the other hand, had an unwieldy hierarchy. The governor-general and an official called the intendant, in charge of economic and commercial affairs, were supposed to share power at the top. But most of the time during the history of New France, these office holders disliked each other and did very little to cooperate even in times of war.

Although the governor-general controlled New France's militia, the commander of France's regular military

"To The Uttermost Of My Power"

detachment, soldiers like the Marquis de Montcalm, retained their autonomy and would let troops take part in military activity only if he agreed with the strategy.

The French made a difficult situation even more confusing with their chains of command. For example, the governor-generals reported to the French Ministry of the Marine; the military generals reported to the French Ministry of War. Oftentimes these two ministers were rivals and they were reluctant to share information or coordinate activities.

In addition, their strongest allies -- the Abenaki, Algonquin, and Huron Indians tribes -- were extremely difficult to restrain, and they would willingly abandon an attack or battle if they appeared to be losing or if they had any disagreement with the French.

Finally, Dominican priests and Jesuit missionaries held strong control over the Indians, and these clerics also wielded -- or at least attempted to wield -- ecclesiastical control over the colonial government, much as they did in France.

Not to be outdone, France's Navy also acted autonomously and officers in Paris often did not agree with the military strategy proposed in Quebec. There was little sense of unified command. In addition, English ships could safely scatter to dozens of ports along the Atlantic coast; French ships had but one place to go -- Louisbourg.

To the English, Louisbourg seemed like a mortal threat, a sword aimed at the heart of their existence. A fortress in Quebec was one thing, New England felt, but one on Cape Breton Island was totally different. It was a

"To The Uttermost Of My Power"

brooding threat to their trade and their safety and security. It was, to use 20th century analogy, just like missiles in Cuba. Surely military leaders in England could understand the threat posed by Louisbourg. But England had bigger concerns than Louisbourg.

At least one New England leader realized that if New England wanted to destroy Louisbourg, New England would have to do it herself.

His name was William Shirley.

"To The Uttermost Of My Power"

Chapter VII

"A Mad Scheme"

FRANCIS PARKMAN CALLED THE PROPOSAL TO ATTACK LOUISBOURG "A MAD SCHEME" -- A NAME THAT MAY WELL HAVE BEEN AN AMAZING UNDERSTATEMENT.

The thought of an amateur Army made up of farmers, mechanics, dockworkers and sailors going to conquer a fortress like Louisbourg was insane.[17]

Nevertheless, that was the goal and the objective of the New England colonies. Ever since the first stone was laid at Louisbourg, the northern British colonies clamored for its destruction. When hostilities between France and England broke out again, the Provincials focused their sites on the fortress.

It is difficult now, looking backward, to determine who first had the idea to attack Louisbourg. William Vaughn, the son of a former lieutenant governor of New Hampshire born in Portsmouth, and a boisterous resident of the Damariscotta region in Maine, claimed it was his idea. Robert Achmuty, a judge of the admiralty in Massachusetts is mentioned as a potential source; Samuel Waldo, Pepperrell's old friend now living on Maine's Casco Bay, also made a paternal claim on the idea. Another claimant was Lt. Colonel John Bradstreet, one of the field grade officers who were victorious at Louisbourg and another close friend of Pepperrell's.[18] As

---

[17] Parkman, Francis, *A Half Century of Conflict*, p. 606.
[18] Parkman, p. 617.

"To The Uttermost Of My Power"

the proverb says: Victory has a thousand fathers, but defeat is an orphan.

No matter who had the idea, the plan to assault Louisbourg was nurtured, protected, promoted, and given shape by the Royal Governor of the Massachusetts colony, Sir William Shirley. If Governor Shirley was not the father of the mad scheme, he certainly was the midwife who gave life to the project and turned it into a reality.

William Shirley was a native Englishman, born in London in 1694. He attended Cambridge University, where he trained to become a lawyer. In 1731, he immigrated to Boston, like many other young men and women, hoping to seek his fortune in the new and more forgiving world of the colonies.

Shirley quickly jumped into the world of Massachusetts politics. He was appointed to a number of Royal posts in the colony, including that of Surveyor of the King's Woods. In this role, he traveled through the northern territories of the colony -- essentially the Province of Maine -- and it was during these visits that he developed an acute understanding of the concerns of those people living on the frontier. He also ran into a local judge in Maine by the name of William Pepperrell when he served as lawyer for the defense in the 1734 case of Frost v. Leighton.

Shirley also served as Advocate General before he reached the pinnacle and was appointed Royal Governor in 1741. He succeeded Jonathan Belcher, who had longstanding struggles with the General Court and the Governor's Council, largely over his salary. When Shirley came to the governor's office, he found he could

"To The Uttermost Of My Power"

work very well with the president or chairman of the Council -- William Pepperrell. In fact, Pepperrell seemed to be everywhere. He was a key leader of commercial life in New England with his fleet of ships sailing the profitable trade routes. He was an effective political leader thanks to his service in the colonial legislature. He was respected in the legal community due to his tenure on the bench. He commanded probably the most important militia in the colony. He had no enemies. He was, Shirley was learning, a man to reckon with.

In spite of the sometimes cutthroat undercurrents of Massachusetts colonial politics, the two men seemed to get along. Shortly after taking office, Shirley accompanied Pepperrell on a tour of York County defensive emplacements. The chief executive came back from that tour totally satisfied with the work and with Pepperrell as commander of the militia.

William Shirley quickly learned how interconnected some of the great colonial families were. In trying to develop a close relationship with Samuel Waldo, he came to know Waldo's brother-in-law from Rhode Island, Nathaniel Sparhawk. Then Shirley was astonished to discover that young Sparhawk was the soon-to-be son-in-law of none other than William Pepperrell. And on top of that, Pepperrell's son would become engaged to Waldo's daughter!

Colonial New England was a very small world.

SHIRLEY HAD BEEN THE LEADER OF A GROUP of politicians who had worked hard to remove the previous governor, Jonathan Belcher. Shirley knew that Pepperrell was a friend of Belcher, but most of the time, the Kittery man steered an even course between the two sides. Shirley

"To The Uttermost Of My Power"

felt he could work with Pepperrell, but he proceeded with much caution.

It is nearly impossible to imagine the influence William Pepperrell wielded in Massachusetts political, economic, judicial, military, social and religious circles. He never grabbed for power because it somehow was always handed to him. Yet he never tried to abuse it. He had seemingly no ambition -- unlike Governor Shirley -- and definitely no enemies.

As governor, Shirley got regular reports from London on the prospects of war. England fought Spain in the latter 1730s, but the colonies were spared because France was not involved. By early 1744, it seemed only a matter of time before hostilities would start with France. Warnings were sent to frontier towns, militia troops trained hurriedly on dusty town greens. Gunpowder and shot were stored away, and town ramparts, stockades and garrison houses were reinforced and modernized. New troops were raised, and ships gathered to form a rudimentary Navy.

Then on May 12, 1744, a ship arrived in Boston from Glasgow, Scotland, carrying with it the news that France and England were at war again, this time in the War of the Austrian Succession.

That same day, a small French flotilla from Louisbourg commanded by Francois Du Pont Duvivier, Governor of Louisbourg, sailed from the fortress to attack the English settlement at Canso. That fishing village quickly surrendered. Canso or Canseaux, was a small fishing outpost on the strait that separates Cape Breton Island and the mainland of Nova Scotia. The French eventually released the captured fishermen from Canso, and many

"To The Uttermost Of My Power"

of them made their way to Boston, where they spread and amplified the tales of their defeat and captivity.

By August, the hostilities continued as a French and Indian force tried unsuccessfully to capture Annapolis Royal in Nova Scotia -- the former French colony of Acadia. In answer to these attacks, Shirley recruited new troops to relieve Annapolis Royal. At the same time, he became convinced New England must conquer and destroy Louisbourg, just like Rome had destroyed its Mediterranean rival -- Carthage.

One disturbing fact reported to Boston was that the Nova Scotia Indian tribes were actively allied with the French in attacking local English settlements. To avoid Indian problems in Maine and northern New England, Shirley called on the colony's chief Indian negotiator for help. William Pepperrell again answered the call.

Pepperrell had been involved in negotiations with the Indian tribes as a negotiator for some time, and it seemed to fit in well with his militia responsibilities. In November of 1744, he traveled deep into Maine to meet with the Penobscot Indians -- a strong branch of the dominant Abenaki tribe. He spoke to them in terms of fidelity and friendship and asked that they keep peace with their English brothers. His questions were answered by the chiefs in a letter he received after his return to Boston. They promised to keep the peace -- and they did.

Shirley was worried about the fall of Canso and the attack on Annapolis Royal was bothersome. He worried that French ships out of Louisbourg would disrupt or destroy the New England fisheries off the Grand Banks, and he feared French privateers from the fortress could

"To The Uttermost Of My Power"

disrupt or eliminate the merchant trade. Worst of all, he feared a French fleet would appear off nearly defenseless Boston to devastate the city. And the blame for all or any of these things could be directed right at Louisbourg.

The Governor pondered the situation and reflected on the thoughts and ideas of Vaughn, Bradstreet and Waldo and how Louisburg threatened the safety of their colonies. Shirley determined to do something about it.

ON JANUARY 7, 1745, SHIRLEY PROPOSED THE LOUISBOURG VENTURE -- THE MAD SCHEME -- IN SECRET TO THE GENERAL Court. He asked for the authority to raise a force of 3,000 men to attack and lay siege to Louisbourg. The General Court took his plan and referred it to a committee, which debated the idea, but sent it back to the governor unapproved. The committee felt the plan would be too expensive and would have little chance of success.

From all accounts, Pepperrell was not in Boston at that time, and he had no impact on the initial rejection by the General Court and the Governor's Council.

Shirley was not about to give up on the scheme, by any means. He felt that public opinion was changing as more prisoners from the Canso defeat arrived in Boston and told their stories. Shirley had several allies in the General Court propose the Louisbourg attack again by petition. They did, but again it was referred to a committee.

This time Pepperrell was in Boston, and when the idea was sent to committee, he was named the panel's chairman. This panel took the proposal under advisement and studied it for several days before giving

"To The Uttermost Of My Power"

it their approval. Pepperrell's committee not only approved the plan, it even increased the size of the Army to 4,500 men.

A grateful Shirley now presented the plan once more in secret to the General Court. With Pepperrell's support, the colonial assembly approved the plan.

The vote tally by the General Court is not known for certain, but Boston legend says the scheme passed by a single vote. The legend also says that the plan would have been defeated had not a General Court member with a broken leg hobbled into the chamber to cast the deciding vote while in a cast.[19]

Word of the plan got out to the public, so the story goes, when a devout member of the General Court apparently was in his boarding house praying for the success of the project when, in conversation with Divine Providence, he blurted out the secret. Someone else heard him through the thin walls of his room and the news spread through and beyond the colonies like wildfire.

While this story is probably fiction, the plan of attack on Louisbourg would be no secret once recruiting and troop movements began. French spies no doubt got the word back to "les francais" waiting in the north.

THIS ASSAULT ON LOUISBOURG WOULD NOT BE THE FIRST EXAMPLE OF A MARTIAL MASSACHUSETTS LEADING MEN OFF TO FIGHT WITH THE FRENCH. In April of 1690, a force raised from the local population boarded ships and left Boston under the command of its then-governor, Sir William Phips -- another native of Maine. The objective

---
[19] Parkman, p. 623.

"To The Uttermost Of My Power"

of this armed flotilla was to capture Port Royal, the capital of Acadia, now known as Annapolis Royal, capital of Nova Scotia.

The Massachusetts troops rolled through the French defenses and defenders so quickly and easily that the New Englanders turned their thoughts to the ultimate target -- Quebec, the capital of New France.

Phips was a giant of a man, standing well over six feet, eight inches tall, and he was the 26th and last child in a family that clung to its land on the coast of Maine, near the present-day site of Phippsburg. He made his fortune in life when he discovered a sunken Spanish treasure ship in the Caribbean and recovered chest after chest of plate gold and silver, as well as bags of gold coins. By the time he and his partners split the treasure -- and after taking out a plentiful share for the Crown of England -- there was only 16,000 pounds left for Phips. But he invested his money and his efforts wisely and the treasure hunter was eventually named governor of his home colony.

He was an enthusiastic and energetic governor and, by most accounts, a popular one. As governor, Phips finally cleaned up the terrifying remnants left behind after the infamous Salem witch trials. He declared the persecutions over, freed any accused witches or victims left in jail, and pledged he would never allow such horrors to happen again.

At Quebec, Phips got the feeling the Provincials might have bitten off more than they could chew. Sitting high on its great rock hundreds of feet above the St. Lawrence, Quebec looked impregnable. And New France's governor-general, Louis de Buade, Count

"To The Uttermost Of My Power"

Frontenac, had made Quebec even stronger when he built the first wall to completely enclose the city. The wooden-planked walls linked ten strong defensive locations and provided essential cover for the French marksmen to disrupt any attack. Phips, meanwhile, had his troops look for a place where the Provincials could launch an offensive against the city. The French residents -- "les habitants" -- sat behind their walls, watched the English, and waited for winter.

Phips had his men look for a weak point in the defenses, and they couldn't find one. He called on Frontenac to surrender, only to have the aging, yet still belligerent, count laughingly decline. Eventually, the Army did make an attempt to attack the city, but the French defenders easily repulsed the assault.

As the end of October drew near and swirls of snow flurries dusted the cold decks of the fleet, Phips knew the geography of Quebec had defeated him. He would not risk more men on another futile attack. The fleet weighed anchor and made for a much friendlier Boston.

Another expedition against New France took place in 1711 during Queen Anne's War. Five regiments of British regulars were to join with some 4,000 colonial troops to attack Montreal by land via Lake Champlain and at the same time Quebec by way of the St. Lawrence River. Commanded by General Francis Nicholson, the only success this enterprise encountered was the capture, for the third time, of Port Royal, the capital of Acadia. The conquerors renamed the city Annapolis Royal, to honor Queen Anne and they decided this time they would not return it to the French.

"To The Uttermost Of My Power"

THE PHIPS AND NICHOLSON EXPEDITIONS AND SHIRLEY'S PROPOSED ATTACK ON LOUISBOURG WERE DEFINITELY A different way for the New England colonies to deal with the French. In the past, militias were used mainly for defensive purposes only; the offensive attacks were always handled by regular English Army troops from Great Britain. Most of the time, the colonial militia was used to garrison forts throughout the colonies.

But the "mad scheme" was different.

Again, Great Britain would foot the bill (Shirley hoped), but New England men would make up the army; New England officers would lead them; and New England governors -- led by Massachusetts -- would devise the strategy. This would not be an English attack -- it would be an attack by New England, by Americans. They would bring the fight directly to the French.

The plan allowed Shirley to raise the funds needed to procure and arm up to 4,000 volunteers from the colonies of Massachusetts, New Hampshire, Connecticut and Rhode Island. Shirley also could appropriate armed vessels owned by the colonies and form them into a naval fighting force to escort army transports to Louisbourg. He also would select the commander of the entire enterprise.

Once the proposal became public, Shirley was overwhelmed by people wanting to command the army. Some of the would-be generals included William Vaughn; Lt. Colonel John Bradstreet, who was well-known in Boston; Benning Wentworth, the Governor of New Hampshire; and many others. Shirley was tempted to take command himself, but he realized someone needed to stay behind in Boston to manage the entire war effort

"To The Uttermost Of My Power"

and there was only one person he could trust with that job -- he, himself.

Unfortunately, very few Provincials had real military experience. They were merchants, lawyers, farmers, printers and craftsmen. They certainly were not soldiers. Shirley himself didn't have the right background. What he needed was a competent general -- really a manager -- who could command an army and undertake the expedition, be popular enough to raise the funds and troops, be pliant enough to follow orders, be good enough not to lose in battle; and be modest enough not to take all the glory.

After evaluating the candidates, Shirley realized there was only one man who could fit that profile and not be a controversial choice. William Pepperrell.

Shirley already knew it was Pepperrell's support that got the plan through the legislature. The Kittery man knew it too, writing shortly after the surrender of Louisbourg in his report: "It must be confessed that would have been no Expedition against this place had I not undertook it." [20]

WHEN SHIRLEY APPROACHED HIM ABOUT THE COMMAND, PEPPERRELL INITIALLY WAS NOT EAGER TO TAKE IT. His wife, Mary, had been sick, and he was reluctant to leave her alone for an unspecified period of time. He was also unsure about his business. Andrew had just become a full partner in the operation, but Pepperrell was not yet

---

[20] Sir William Pepperrell to Henry Stafford, 4 November 1745, Miscellaneous Collections, Massachusetts Historical Society, Boston, Massachusetts.

"To The Uttermost Of My Power"

sure his son was ready to take over total control, and that would be the case if he took command of the army.

Always a realist, Pepperrell also had some major doubts about his military potential. It was true he had headed the militia for a long time, but he knew there was a big difference between reviewing troops and inspecting fortifications and leading a real army against a location as strong as Louisbourg.

Pepperrell's only real military experience had occurred during Queen Anne's War when he served as a teen-age sentry at the old Fort William site in Kittery Point.

When Pepperrell received word from Shirley about the command, he had a special guest visiting him at the family home. Rev. George Whitefield was a prominent New England preacher who helped revive spirituality in the region as part of the phenomenon known as the "Great Awakening." Other ministers associated with this revival-like focus on religion were Jonathan Edwards, Cotton and Increase Mather, and Pepperrell's own preacher at the Kittery Point church, Rev. John Newmarch.[21]

---

[21] Not much is known about Rev. Newmarch's background. He graduated from Harvard College in 1690 and began his pastoral career in Kittery shortly thereafter. At that time, Kittery consisted of five parishes and he served them all. He was hired by the town on a year-to-year basis, until November 1, 1714, when he was hired by the 13 founding members of the First Congregational Church in Kittery Point. He was ordained shortly thereafter. He remained in that church for the rest of his preaching career until he retired in 1751. He died and was buried in Kittery in 1754.

"To The Uttermost Of My Power"

It seems Rev. Whitefield discouraged Pepperrell from taking the command. He told Pepperrell failure in this enterprise would condemn and ruin him, while success would only increase the envy and jealousy people already felt toward him. Pepperrell delayed his decision.

In the meantime, word of the proposed expedition was spreading like wildfire throughout the New England colonies. Preachers took to their pulpits and roared out condemnations of the Catholic French and their godless savage Indian allies.

Not all voices were that optimistic about the chance for success. A young printer in Philadelphia wrote his elder brother in Boston: "Fortified towns are hard nuts to crack, and your teeth are not accustomed to it." Then Benjamin Franklin added "but some think they are as easily taken as snuff."[22]

Ever-eager, ever-anxious, Governor Shirley wanted an answer. He confronted Pepperrell and told him he was "indispensable" for success.

Finally, after long discussions with family, friends and military acquaintances in Boston, Pepperrell made up his mind and decided to take command. He became an instant lieutenant general.

Governor Shirley already had permission to build his army; now he had a general to command it.

---

[22] Parkman, p. 621.

"To The Uttermost Of My Power"

Chapter VIII

New England Unites

WILLIAM PEPPERRELL WAS THE RIGHT CHOICE TO COMMAND THE LOUISBOURG EXPEDITION. NOT A SOUL IN HIGH PLACES RAISED AN OBJECTION, AND THE REST OF THE NEW ENGLAND GOVERNORS HAD NO PROBLEM WITH SHIRLEY'S SELECTION.

That vote of confidence also satisfied the Duke of Newcastle, King George's Secretary of State for Great Britain, who effectively ruled the British Empire. Born Thomas Pelham Holles, the Duke was a member of the land-holding aristocracy and early on devoted his life to government service. King George I in 1715 elevated Holles to the dukedom and then named him to the Secretary of State's office; a job he held for the next 30 years.

Local officials throughout New England lauded Pepperrell's selection, and he heard lots of positive commentary from some important religious leaders throughout the region, including his wife's relative, the Rev. Samuel Moody of York, Maine. Rev. Moody not only approved of the choice of commander, he volunteered to go on the expedition as a chaplain to minister to the spiritual needs of the soldiers.

Moody, who Pepperrell came to know quite well over the years, was planning to make the upcoming military effort into a true "crusade" against the Papist French to the north. He would bring a huge axe with him on the

"To The Uttermost Of My Power"

expedition; it would be useful, he told anyone who would listen, in hacking to pieces any Catholic altars he should find at Louisbourg.

The almost universal acceptance and approval of Pepperrell was key to Shirley's choice. New England was no happy family of colonies; men from Massachusetts didn't like New Hampshire men and vice versa; no one liked Rhode Islanders, and the Connecticut contingent would be a true wild card. Shirley also felt Pepperrell could deal effectively with the Royal Navy if he could get the fleet's support for the campaign. He needed a congenial man, yet a determined man. Shirley hoped he had chosen the right man.

Pepperrell also received congratulatory letters from most of his would-be-rivals for command, including the volatile William Vaughn, his friend John Bradstreet, and even Benning Wentworth.

BENNING WENTWORTH HAD BECOME ROYAL GOVERNOR OF NEW HAMPSHIRE IN 1741 when that colony once again became its own royal administrative unit. Wentworth succeeded his father, John, who had been lieutenant governor when Massachusetts and New Hampshire were combined under a single official.

Before he assumed the Royal governorship, Benning Wentworth had been a trading rival of William Pepperrell's, sending similar cargoes to similar ports where they tried to outdo each other.

Once he became a Royal official, Wentworth quickly developed a reputation for corruption. He enriched himself by selling disputed land in what is now Vermont in spite of protests by New York, which also claimed the

"To The Uttermost Of My Power"

Green Mountain land. He named settlements after his patrons -- Rutland was named for the third duke of Rutland and Bennington was named after himself. He was the constant butt of jokes by ordinary citizens as demonstrated by Kenneth Roberts in his great novel about the French and Indian War, *Northwest Passage*.

A commercial rivalry between a Pepperrell and a Wentworth was nothing new in the Piscataqua region. Before he took office, Benning's father John was a sailing captain who worked for Colonel Pepperrell. For some reason now lost to history, they had a falling out and Wentworth went on to use his talents to obtain the top Royal appointment in New Hampshire. It soon became clear that Wentworth was not above using his position to strike back at his old boss.

Most port collectors and custom officials would look the other way at some smuggling activities. But in Pepperrell's case, the New Hampshire officials were especially diligent. In fact, more than once not only did Wentworth seize cargoes, but the ships were embargoed as well, causing the elder Pepperrell to go to court to get them back.

When Shirley notified the unsuccessful candidates about the generalship, he got caught in a comedy of errors with Governor Wentworth. He wrote Wentworth and said he regretted the New Hampshire man's gout was so bad he knew he couldn't give him the command. Then Wentworth wrote back his legs were fine, and he would be ready to go at a moment's notice. This forced Shirley to apologize to Wentworth and tell him it was too late to change commanders.

"To The Uttermost Of My Power"

Wentworth did write to congratulate Pepperrell on receiving the command; he also included an offer to sell him a tent for use on campaign. But he would only sell it to him on a personal basis, and not if the army was buying it. Wentworth was no fool; if Pepperrell bought it on his own, Wentworth would be paid right away. If the Army bought it, he might never get paid.

Meanwhile, Pepperrell was focused on the army and making his presence known. When he arrived in Boston, Governor Shirley presented him with three ornately designed military officer commissions, one each from Massachusetts, Connecticut and New Hampshire naming him a lieutenant general from each province.

BY NOW, SHIRLEY AND PEPPERRELL WERE BEGINNING TO BUILD AN ARMY. On January 25, 1745, the General Court did a great deal to help mobilization and enlistment when it passed a bill authorizing the pay for the soldiers. Compensation ranged from 15 pounds a month for a brigadier general to 25 shillings a month for a private soldier. Volunteers were also promised an appropriate amount of "plunder." They also were to receive rations of ginger and sugar; a daily ration of grog or rum and each man would be issued a blanket.

In addition, militia captains who raised companies of 50 men or more were awarded a special bonus. The legislature also created the War Council, a group of legislators to oversee the conduct of the war. Pepperrell also had his own Army war council consisting of himself, Generals Wolcott, Waldo and Dwight, and the regimental commanders. The council would make joint decisions about the campaign once it got under way. But Pepperrell had retained the right to overrule a decision if he felt he should.

"To The Uttermost Of My Power"

Slowly the Army began to take shape. By the time it was finally assembled, Massachusetts had provided 3,300 soldiers, Connecticut 516, New Hampshire 494. Rhode Island promised fighting men, but they never showed up.

Because Connecticut raised so many men, that colony's lieutenant governor, Roger Wolcott, was given the position of deputy commander, or major general. Pepperrell had hoped to have Samuel Waldo as his second-in-command, but Shirley overruled him. Waldo became, instead, one of the two brigadier generals in the army. Pepperrell and Wolcott soon became good friends.

Shirley had asked all colonies north of Virginia to contribute what they could to the war effort. The colony of New York contributed some artillery and siege guns, while New Jersey and Pennsylvania sent supplies and ammunition. The rest sent nothing.

After nearly six weeks of intense recruitment, training and organizing, Pepperrell distributed his Order of Battle to key leaders in Massachusetts and afterwards to the other colonies:

The New England Land Forces, 1745
Lt. General, Wm. Pepperrell, Mass.
Major Gen. Roger Walcott, Conn.
Brigadier Gen. Samuel Waldo, Mass.
Brigadier Gen. Joseph Dwight, Mass.

Regiments:
Massachusetts
Pepperrell's Reg., Lt. Col. Bradstreet
Waldo's Reg., Lt. Col. Noble
Dwight's Reg., Lt. Col. Thomas
Moulton's Reg., Lt. Col. Donnell

"To The Uttermost Of My Power"

Willard's Reg., Lt. Col. Chandler
Hale's Reg., Lt. Col. Everleigh
Richmond's Reg., Lt. Col. Pitts
Connecticut
Wolcott's Reg., Lt. Col. Burr
New Hampshire
Gorham's Reg., Lt. Col. Gorham
Moore's Reg., Lt. Col. Meserve

Artillery
Lt. Col. Gridley

Escort Fleet
Captain Edward Tyng[23]

The Pepperrell name was helping to fill in the ranks in those regiments. In Kittery, 115 men volunteered for a 50-man company going on the Louisbourg expedition. South Berwick, at one time part of Kittery land grant, sent the same number of soldiers without Pepperrell even having to ask. Major John Storer of the Maine militia earned the bonus when he raised a company of 61 men, ranging in age from 60 to 16, in a single day.

At the same time, the General Court was passing resolutions allowing Shirley to requisition armed sailing ships from the colonies to form a colonial navy; to gather the transports needed to get the army to Louisbourg; to arrange for clothing, uniforms, and weapons for the troops; and to allow Governor Shirley to ask the home government in England to pay for everything.

Thanks to his purchasing power, Shirley became a very popular man with the merchants and outfitters of

---

[23] Parsons, p. 347.

"To The Uttermost Of My Power"

Boston. They had lots to supply -- blankets, uniforms, small arms and food. A great deal of food; enough food to feed a 4,500-man army three times a day for at least several months. One of the major recipients of Shirley's largesse in awarding contracts was the trading firm headed by Thomas Hancock. It is believed the Hancock's profited by nearly 12,000 pounds English money in supplying the New England Land Forces. By the 1760's, this company was headed by Thomas's successor, John Hancock, the future president of the Second Continental Congress and the most prominent signer of the Declaration of Independence.

The letter-writing Shirley then turned his pen to naval affairs. He asked the lords of the Admiralty in London for the help of the Royal Navy in conquering Louisbourg. Shirley had recruited a colonial armed flotilla under Captain Edward Tyng of Massachusetts, but he wanted professional Navy ships to counter the French fleet they might face off of Canada. Just in case London rejected his request, Shirley also wrote to Commodore Peter Warren, commanding the Royal Navy's North American station, to see if he could spare some ships.

Lt. General Pepperrell, meanwhile, was bombarded with letters, memos, suggestions, orders and prayers -- many of them from William Shirley. It was obvious Shirley wanted the command, and he seemed very frustrated by the time it took to get the army ready. He sent Pepperrell precise plans of attack, even though neither man had ever been to Louisboug. The plans were so detailed they even included the proposed time for the assaults to take place.

One of Shirley's favorite plans called for the army to arrive in the middle of the night, unload nearly 100 ships

"To The Uttermost Of My Power"

filled with men and heavy artillery with no lights, organize formations and march on the fortress by sunrise. Pepperrell read the orders, realized they were well-intentioned but impractical, and then filed them away.

Pepperrell had spent much of the time since his appointment shuttling back and forth between Boston and Kittery, getting his business under son Andrew's control for the duration of the war, and making sure his military details were handled. In addition, his wife Mary was still recuperating from her illness, and he tried to spend as much time with her as he could.

By the end of March -- in little more than eight weeks -- the army was ready, and Pepperrell and his commanders began to load men and equipment into the holds of nearly 100 ships to be used as transports and troop carriers. Already on board were the large siege artillery -- cannon and mortars -- that would be needed to breech the thick walls of Louisbourg. The cannon would be used to directly batter down the walls; the mortars would lob large shells and solid shot onto and over the walls to do their destructive work. Deep in the holds were the wooden flat bottom boats that would be used to land the New England troops.

As one writer put it years later, the Louisbourg expedition was a plan drawn up by a lawyer, led by a merchant, carried out by farmers and fisherman and all aimed at a fortress considered impregnable by experts. Others likened the expedition to a large camping trip that happened to have a military objective.

IN 1833, NATHANIEL HAWTHORNE, THE GREAT AMERICAN MAN OF LETTERS FROM NEW ENGLAND, penned a

"TO THE UTTERMOST OF MY POWER"

fascinating tribute to Sir William Pepperrell in one of his sketches of heroic New Englanders.

As Hawthorne described it: "He was a famous general, the most prominent military character in our ante-Revolutionary annals and he may be taken as the representative of a class of warriors peculiar to their age and country -- true citizen-soldiers, who diversified a life of commerce or agriculture by the episode of a city sacked, or a battle won, and, having stamped their names on the page of history, went back to the routine of peaceful occupation."[24]

Hawthorne then describes Pepperrell's departure with the fleet on March 29, 1745, as the armada got under way. He focuses on the arrival of a group that includes Pepperrell and Shirley.

> It is a bright and breezy day in March, and about twenty small white clouds are scudding seaward before the wind, airy forerunners of the fleet of privateers and transports that spread their sails to the sunshine of the harbor. The time is at its height and the gunwales of a barge alternately rise above the wharf, and then sinks from view, as it lies rocking on the waves in readiness to convey the general and his suite on board the Shirley galley . . .
>
> Next appear six figures who demand our more minute attention. He in the center is the general, a well-proportioned man, with a slight hoar-frost of age just visible on him, he views the fleet in which he is about to embark with no stronger expression than a calm anxiety, as if he were sending a freight of his own merchandise to Europe. A scarlet British uniform, made of the best broadcloth imported by himself, adorns the person, and in the left pocket of a large

---

[24] Hawthorne, Nathaniel, "*Sir William Pepperrell*", 1833. Elditch.com. (Online), 2007.

"To The Uttermost Of My Power"

> buff waistcoat, near the pommel of the sword, we see the protuberance of a small Bible, which certainly may benefit his pious soul, and, perchance may protect his body from a bullet.
>
> The middle-aged gentleman . . . in silk, gold, and velvet, and with a pair of spectacles thrust above his forehead, is Governor Shirley. The quick motion of his small eyes in their puckered sockets, his grasp on one of the general's bright military buttons, the gesticulation of his forefinger, keeping time with the earnest rapidity of his words, have all something characteristic. His mind is calculated to fill up the wild conceptions of other men with its own minute ingenuities; and he seeks, as it were, to climb up to the moon by piling pebble-stones one upon another. He is now impressing on the general's recollection the voluminous details of a plan for surprising Louisburg in the depth of midnight, and thus to finish the campaign within twelve hours after the arrival of the troops.[25]

Sometime around four in the afternoon, Lt. General Pepperrell gave orders to the ships in Nantasket Roads -- a mooring spot some five miles south of Boston -- to weigh anchor, and sailors on the transports and fighting ships got the fleet underway.

AS PEPPERRELL LED THE INVASION FLEET NORTH TO CAPE BRETON ISLAND, another naval force was weighing anchor far to the south in the Caribbean. Commodore Peter Warren was leaving Antigua to bring three of his Royal Navy fighting ships north to Louisbourg to support Pepperrell's effort. Warren had received the letter from Governor Shirley asking for assistance. His first instinct had been to move north quickly, but he dared not leave his post unless the Admiralty gave its approval. Warren, a native of Ireland, had married a colonial, and he had great sympathy with the New England effort.

---

[25] Hawthorne.

"To The Uttermost Of My Power"

So Warren was a happy man when an Admiralty dispatch arrived giving him permission to leave. But it arrived only two days after he sent a message to Shirley announcing that he wouldn't come. Warren's appearance to the north would be a pleasant surprise to Shirley and Pepperrell.

As Warren and his three ships, the *Superb*, 60 guns, the *Mermaid* and the *Launceton* -- both 40 guns -- beat their way north toward Boston, they met a packet ship that had recently left the city.

Francis Parkman, in his *A Half Century of Conflict,* said the captain told Warren that Pepperrell's fleet had already left for Louisbourg. Warren then determined to bypass the capital and set sail directly for Cape Breton Island.

The mad scheme was underway.

MEANWHILE, THE OBJECT OF ALL THIS ATTENTION LAY QUIETLY UNDER THE EARLY SPRING CANADIAN SUN. LOUISBOURG WAS PEACEFUL EVEN AS GUARDS AND LOOKOUTS searched the horizon for a mast or sail. Relief and re-supply were said to be on the way from France, and the garrison hoped to see King Louis XV's flag crest the horizon before that of George II.

The French knew the "Bastonais" -- the Bostonians -- were coming. All of North America seemed to know they were coming, and they were coming to Louisbourg. During the first two colonial wars, it was usually the French who attacked the English. Now the English specifically New England -- were coming at them. They knew Governor Shirley was raising an army to reduce

"To The Uttermost Of My Power"

their stronghold. They knew time was running out, but all the French leaders did was hold councils.

France was stretched too thin around the world, and Louis XV was too embroiled in Europe to worry much about New France. France was encircled by enemy alliances and besides fighting in Europe, the French possessions in India were at stake, and they were more valuable and lucrative than Canada ever would be. New France had always protected itself before; it would have to do so again.

The Governor of Louisbourg -- the Marquis Louis DuPont Duchambon -- was in position by the accident of death -- the death of his predecessor, the Marquis DuQuestral. The late marquis was the one who ordered his forces to drive the English out of Canso when the war had begun. He had died of fever during the winter, leaving responsibility for the entire region to the inexperienced Duchambon.

As a result of DuQuestral's death and the overall lack of planning by the French, Duchambon had less than 500 regular troops to defend the fortress and man the guns. Many of these troops had mutinied during the previous winter when they were willfully denied their rightful rations of food and clothing. Even if the regiments were at full strength, there wouldn't have been enough to man the walls. Louisbourg's militia strength was never high because of New France's small population.

Another force of French and Indians was in the vicinity. Led by the partisan leader Colonel Michel de Bourtz Marin, this force was sent by the Quebec government to help in the siege of Annapolis Royal. When the British lifted that siege, Marin fell back on Cape Breton Island.

"To The Uttermost Of My Power"

According to French records, Duchambon was not the most political and polished of governors. He alienated many people and it surprised none of the other Canadian officials when the troops mutinied in the winter. He was strident, loud, foolish and unpopular. He was not the type of leader to inspire a last stand. His Army was demoralized; he had no naval force either, not even privateers that could counter the English ships that haunted the outer harbors. And with no naval protection, there were no ships and therefore no hope.

"To The Uttermost Of My Power"

Chapter IX

New England Has Arrived

BY FOUR PM, ALL THE DIGNITARIES FROM BOSTON WERE SAFELY ASHORE AND THE SHIPS WERE UNDERWAY AND DISAPPEARING OVER THE HORIZON.

Wandering on the edges of the fleet, like border collies herding their flocks, were the 13 fighting ships of the Tyng battle squadron donated by the New England colonies. Captain Edward Tyng of Massachusetts commanded this flotilla, and he was charged with guiding the fleet safely to Cape Breton Island.

Tyng's colonial battle squadron included the *Shirley*, 24 guns; *Massachusetts*, (frigate) 24 guns; *Molineux*, 20; *Prince of Orange*, 14; *Caesar*, 14; *Fame*, 20; *Boston Packet*, 16; *Tartar*, 14; *Re solution*, 12; *Defence*, 16; *Abigail*, 10; *Bonetta*, 6; *Massachusetts*, (Sloop), 10; and *Lord Montagu*, 10.

Within hours, however, the vessels encountered something the planners had not predicted and did not want -- a full-force gale.

For the next day and a half, the gale battered Pepperrell's fleet, scattering them to the four winds. No ships were lost, but several were severely damaged. The fleet rode out the storm, and then most made their way to a pre-assigned rendezvous point.

Two days later, the fleet had reconstituted itself at Sheepscot Bay, midway up the coast of Maine. There

"To The Uttermost Of My Power"

Pepperrell waited while damaged ships were repaired and the sailing crews and soldiers on board regained their sea legs. For many of the volunteer soldiers, this was their first trip to sea and seasickness ran rampant.

Shipwrights accompanying the fleet completed the repair work on any damaged vessels quickly and competently. By early April, the fleet left Sheepscot Bay and turned into the north for Cape Sable. Several ships carrying troops from Connecticut were still missing, but Pepperrell assumed they would catch up en route or meet the fleet at Louisbourg.

On April 4, at about four o'clock in the afternoon, the fleet arrived off Canso, the English fishing village the French captured in 1744. They had met no naval opposition on the voyage, which Pepperrell called, in a letter to the Duke of Newcastle, "rough and somewhat tedious."

The next day, one of Tyng's escort cruisers on patrol ran down and captured a French ship loaded with molasses and other Caribbean items and bound for Louisbourg.

Also that day, Pepperrell convened the first meeting of his War Council to discuss their situation and make plans. The War Council included Pepperrell, his second-in-command Major General Roger Wolcott, Brigadier Generals Samuel Waldo and Joseph Dwight, and the regimental colonels. Other officers attended council meetings when needed. For example, William Vaughn, a colonel of the New Hampshire troops, attended this first meeting. Pepperrell must have had faith in collegial decisions, because sometimes these board meetings included up to 18 participants.

"To The Uttermost Of My Power"

That first meeting resulted in two major decisions. First, they voted to build a blockhouse -- to be called Fort Cumberland in honor of the English duke and son of King George II -- at Canso. Eight cannon and two companies of soldiers totaling 80 men would defend the fort. Even though several troop ships were still missing because of the storm, the council voted that the fleet would leave immediately for Louisbourg.

The council, the fleet and the army, however, would spend the next three weeks at Canso. Three severe snowstorms would strike the Canso area, bringing bitter cold with them, making any fleet movement impossible.

Pepperrell fell ill in the interim and had to stay in bed for several days on board the *Shirley* to recuperate. Even after the snow moderated, the seas around Canso were still full of ice and it made navigating their way safely to Louisbourg impossible. Reports also indicated ice was clogging the proposed landing site at Gabarus Bay. So while the blockhouse was being built, Pepperrell used the time to drill and train the green volunteer troops.

Meanwhile, local residents told the New Englanders about rumors of a large French fleet commanded by the Comte de Maurepas making its way from Europe to Louisbourg. Pepperrell knew that even a small French fleet could wreck havoc among his convoy. His worries mounted almost daily while the fleet remained moored in the ice and fog of Canso.

No doubt Pepperrell was grateful and relieved when, on April 22, ships flying the Union Jack made their way into the harbor. They were ships carrying the missing troops from Connecticut, and accompanying them was the

"To The Uttermost Of My Power"

warship *Eltham*, 40 guns, and detached from the Royal Navy's North American squadron.

The next day dawned even brighter for Pepperrell when three more Royal Navy ships sailed into the harbor. They were the vessels under Commodore Peter Warren that had left Antigua the same day Pepperrell left Boston.

Lt. General Pepperrell was elated.

On the day they set sail from Boston, Governor Shirley had indicated that the Royal Navy would not be available to assist the expedition. But Shirley had been wrong and now Pepperrell had four heavily gunned Royal Navy ships to protect the transport fleet and to blockade Louisbourg.

Commodore Warren, however, was in a hurry and didn't have time to come aboard the *Shirley* and meet with Pepperrell. So he and the General exchanged letters, and the Commodore left for Louisbourg to begin the blockade of the port. Pepperrell would follow with the army when it was ready.

Born in Ireland in 1703, Warren was the youngest son of Michael Warren and Catherine Plunkett, born Aylmer. His uncle was Michael Aylmer, baron, admiral and commander-in-chief, who had entered the Navy under the sponsorship of the Duke of Buckingham as a lieutenant, in 1678.

Warren joined the Royal Navy as an ordinary seaman in Dublin in 1716 when he was just 13 years old. Warren was fortunate that his talents were noted, and he swiftly rose in the ranks, becoming a captain in 1727.

"To The Uttermost Of My Power"

In 1731, he married Susannah Delancey, whose brother James was the chief justice and lieutenant governor of New York.

Over the years, Warren acquired several thousand acres of land on the south side of the Mohawk River in the New York colony. He hired his nephew, from Ireland, William Johnson, to manage these western lands, and Johnson went on to become the chief Indian agent in British North America as well as a victorious general.

In 1744, Warren was made commodore and given command of a 16-ship squadron off the Leeward Islands in the Caribbean. While in the Caribbean, Warren and his squadron captured a number of enemy war and cargo ships, many of them laden with rich goods being sent home from the Far East. He and many of his men became rich from this legalized marauding.

On April 23, a very happy Pepperrell wrote to Warren:

> Dear Sir,
>
> I heartily congratulate you on your arrival with your squadron, the advice of which, by your favor of this day, gives me great pleasure. I am confidant that nothing which the strictest vigilance and prudence can foresee or bravery executed will be wanting on your part, and doubt not you will succeed in preventing the introduction of provisions and succors into Louisbourg, and that we shall soon have the pleasure of a meeting there.
>
> Wm. Pepperrell, Lt. General[26]

The next day, Commodore Warren's ships were cruising off Louisbourg, looking for prizes. One of the first things

---

[26] Parsons, Pepperrell to Warren, April 23, 1745, p. 58.

"To The Uttermost Of My Power"

his squadron did was to drive off a French frigate trying to re-supply Louisbourg. It would be one of the last ships to try to break the blockade.

On April 29, Pepperrell, who had divided his fleet into four divisions, ordered the fleet to weigh anchor and ordered his helmsmen to steer for Louisbourg, about 50 miles away. He also sent 270 New Hampshire men aboard an armed sloop to attack and destroy the small French fishing village of St. Peter's on Cape Breton Island. They drove off the inhabitants, destroyed fishing boats and burned the stockade there. Then they too sailed for Louisbourg.

Meanwhile, the French knew the "Bastonais" had left Boston and were on their way. The garrison's great hope was that the Comte de Maurepas and his fleet from France would get there first. This fleet was one of their few remaining hopes for salvation.

As the sun rose on April 30th, French lookouts were scanning the early morning sky when suddenly a forest of masts broke over the horizon. They seemed innumerable, and even more continued to appear. Was it the entire French Navy coming to their rescue?

For several minutes, the lookouts watched the ships closely to see if they could recognize a flag. Eyes strained through spyglasses, until one of them shouted "Alors, mes amis, c'est les Bastonias!"

New England had arrived.

"To The Uttermost Of My Power"

Chapter X

The Siege Of Louisbourg

SO FAR SO GOOD.

That would have been an appropriate conclusion for Pepperrell to make now that the fleet had made it safely to Louisbourg, the Royal Navy was there to support them, and the weather was beginning to cooperate.

But the three-week sojourn at Canso revealed to Pepperrell several weaknesses that might eventually plague the New England Army. Some of the equipment, such as muskets and cannon, were defective; the stores seemed inadequate; and he feared he might have to abandon a long siege if food gave out.

Food was already beginning to spoil, causing Pepperrell and the men to curse the commissaries who had supplied the regiments. Daily rations were typical of military food at the times -- about a pound of salt pork, beef, or bacon per day, with flour, dried corn or peas, sugar and tea, along with the daily ration of grog, which was liquor, usually rum. (Thus the derivation of the word groggy.)

The troops, when they were delayed at Canso, had proven to be unruly and often unwilling to behave and follow orders, especially after receiving their ration of rum. They often ignored their officers and paid no attention to orders if they didn't like them. This was the curse of militia -- and the challenge for Pepperrell.

"To The Uttermost Of My Power"

The General knew he had to get the troops ashore and into action. They had already spent too much time doing nothing. They had come to fight and they needed to engage the French as soon as possible, because the taking of Louisbourg was going to be as difficult as everyone expected it to be. At first glance, Louisbourg looked impregnable.

Francis Parkman described Louisbourg in 1745 as follows: "Louisbourg stood on a tongue of land which lay between its harbor and the sea, and the end of which was prolonged eastward by reefs and shoals that partly barred the entrance to the port, leaving a navigable passage not half a mile wide." This necessary waterway was dominated by a powerful gun emplacement known as the Island Battery that was placed on a small rocky island in the middle of that channel. This battery was designed to provide a withering cross-fire in conjunction with the "Grand" or Royal Battery, a detached work "which stood on the shore of the harbor, opposite the entrance and more than a mile from the town."[27]

In a chest aboard his flagship, Pepperrell kept the large collection of orders, commands, edicts, pleadings and requests from Shirley on how to conduct the upcoming battle. No doubt, the newly minted General appreciated the advice, but he knew that HE was the commander on the scene and he would have to use his best judgment in every battle, every skirmish, and every volley.

The command relationship between Shirley and Pepperrell in 1745 is in many ways similar to the one that existed between American Generals George C. Marshall and Dwight D. Eisenhower 200 years later in

---

[27] Parkman, p. 638-639.

"To The Uttermost Of My Power"

1944. Marshall, as U.S. Army Chief Staff, held a much higher rank than Eisenhower and he indeed was the boss of the Army's war efforts.

General Marshall did the planning for the June 6, 1944 D-Day invasion of Europe and gave all the orders. Eisenhower was charged with implementing those plans and for reporting results to President Franklin D. Roosevelt through General Marshall. Marshall knew the glory would go to the battlefield general and not the planning one -- he even thought of swapping jobs with Eisenhower to take field command in Europe. But President Roosevelt wouldn't let him go. Marshall was correct about the glory -- in 1952, Eisenhower, the battlefield hero, was elected President of the United States. Marshall, who also served as Secretary of State and Secretary of Defense under President Harry S. Truman, went home.

SOON AFTER THE FLEET ARRIVED, THE SHIPS DROPPED ANCHOR IN GABARUS BAY, about three miles west of the city of Louisbourg. Immediately, Pepperrell began unloading men and equipment, ferrying them from ship to shore. As quickly as they could, however, French troops came out of the city to contest the beach at the targeted Flat Point landing area. Pepperrell saw this and decided to try some subterfuge. He ordered some of the boats in toward Flat Point, but had the rest of the boats wait near the transports. When the French moved on the limited landings, Pepperrell ordered the other boats to move in a different direction.

This tactical move allowed the Provincials to came ashore uncontested about two miles up the bay at Freshwater Cove. By the time the French tried to rebuff the landings there, it was too late. The landing site was now well

"To The Uttermost Of My Power"

defended by the Provincials, and more and more boats were landing and strengthening the defending force. By nightfall, half of the New England army was ashore. The rest of the troops landed during the morning hours of the next two days.

Pepperrell's original plan -- agreed upon before he left Boston by the War Council -- called for the army to unload the stores and munitions very quickly and then take the cannon and mortars to a number of positions surrounding the city where batteries would be built. Then the artillery would either batter the city and fortress into submission, or, when the walls were breached by artillery, the infantry would storm the city, and garner victory.

Over the next several days, Pepperrell and his officers worked to assign troop locations in the camp, and to establish a defensive perimeter. The site they chose for the camp was on both sides of a stream that emptied into Freshwater Cove. It was such a good site that General Sir Jeffrey Amherst used it in 1758 when his army laid siege to the fortress.

THEN, TO THE COMPLETE SURPRISE OF EVERYONE, THE NEW ENGLAND LAND FORCES HAD AN AMAZING STROKE OF LUCK.

On May 1, Pepperrell ordered William Vaughn to take 400 men and make an attempt to destroy a series of storehouses near the Royal Battery on the far side of the harbor. Vaughn had some success and buildings were torched, but heavy smoke from the conflagrations forced his detachment to withdraw. By the next morning, the smoke had cleared and visibility was excellent. When Vaughn looked at the Royal Battery, he saw no flag flying there.

"To The Uttermost Of My Power"

Quickly and quietly Vaughn and 13 men approached the Royal Battery on foot. Everything was eerily silent. There was no fire from the ramparts and the portal doors were open. The French were gone! Vaughn and his soldiers quickly deployed throughout the battery to make sure the French had left, and then they made preparations to defend the battery from a counterattack. Vaughn dashed off a note to Pepperrell telling him of his good fortune and asking for assistance to hold the location.

"May it please your Honour," Vaughn wrote the General, "to be informed that by the grace of God and the courage of 13 men, I entered the Royal Battery about 9 o'clock and I am waiting for a reinforcement and a flag."[28]

Vaughn had no flag to fly on the battery flagstaff, so he had William Tufts, an 18 year-old private soldier from Medford, Massachusetts, climb the pole and fasten a red British jacket to it. The jacket would do for now.

Meanwhile, the French tried to correct their blunder and retake the battery. The French counterattack kept Vaughn and his 13 men very busy returning musket fire, until Lt. Colonel John Bradstreet arrived with more soldiers and a Union Jack flag. Bradstreet's men drove off the French, and soon the British flag was waving over the Royal Battery.[29]

Apparently French battery Captain Chassin du Thierry was shaken by the attack on the storehouses and felt the battery was vulnerable, overexposed and couldn't be defended without large loss of life. So he had ordered

---

[28] Parkman, p. 641-642.
[29] Parkman, p. 642.

"To The Uttermost Of My Power"

the guns spiked and the battery abandoned. Now the enemy held it.

The French were in such a hurry to leave they only superficially spiked the guns and the Provincials were able to repair them very quickly. This rapid repair gave Pepperrell an additional supply of ordnance including 28 42-pound cannon and two 18-pound guns, plus a healthy supply of solid round shot for the guns.

Pepperrell ordered troops and munitions into the battery and within hours, the Royal Battery was firing on the city instead of defending it.

Pepperrell had been fortunate so far. His men had landed safely and the Royal Battery was already taken. Now he was determined to press the siege as quickly as possible. He knew that he must set up batteries to pound the town into submission.

But from his camp, General Pepperrell was looking out at a major problem. More than three miles of swamp and marshland stood between the moored fleet and locations near enough to the town to make them a likely site for a battery. The General only hoped his men could drag the cannon through that swampy mess.

First things first, however. The job of unloading and landing the cannon and stores proved difficult, if not impossible. Many of the flat-bottomed boats were smashed on the sides of ships or capsized in the rough spring surf as the unloading work progressed. The water was freezing cold, and it soaked those men working in it. Soon the rough working conditions had many of the men's clothes in tatters.

"To The Uttermost Of My Power"

In addition, there weren't enough tents to go around, forcing the men to use imagination to find shelter. They used old navy sails, any kind of cloth, wood and branches to make lean-tos, make-shift cabins, anything to keep dry and warm during the cold Canadian spring nights.

These conditions made another unwanted thing possible in the camp: disease. Unsanitary conditions, boredom and overexertion made fever possible and typhoid, that scourge of all military encampments, was beginning to spread.

But, as Pepperrell feared, the worst of all undertakings assigned to the soldiers was the effort to bring the cannon across the three miles of marshland that separated the fortress from Gabarus Bay. Cannon sank in the marsh and mud. Sleds brought with them from New England disintegrated into rotting pieces of wood. There were no horses or oxen to pull the cannon into place -- the men were their own beasts of burden. They pulled and pushed guns into place, struggling with the heavy artillery pieces. Finally, they were able to set up a battery of six guns on Green Hill, not far from the King's Bastion, which contained the French headquarters.

Once that battery was ready, Pepperrell and his officers discovered many of his men had no idea how to operate the guns. He sent word to Commodore Warren, asking to borrow several of his Navy gun crews who could teach artillery operational procedures to his men. Warren sent a number of his gun crews ashore to the Army, which received a crash course in gunnery. The siege weapons were now much more accurate and efficient.

"To The Uttermost Of My Power"

Slowly the guns got closer to the battery sites, but it was difficult, relentless, backbreaking work, done under less than favorable conditions. Pepperrell felt his men were doing fine work even though they were working under the most difficult and uncomfortable positions imaginable.

Pepperrell and his men were learning first hand that siege warfare is pure and simple drudgery. Siege warfare was endless work, moving guns, digging trenches, living in dirt and mud, all-night bombardments when no one on either side slept, moving guns again when the range changed -- boring, endless, monotonous, hard work. No charges, no attacks, no glory.

His official report outlined the daily problems faced by the Army. On May 7, the men had to remove several large mortars from the Green Hill Battery because they didn't have enough range to reach the city walls.

On May 11, a battery of four 24-pounders was erected; the next day two of the guns burst while firing on the city, killing several gunners.

"The 15th of May, the thirteen inch mortar burst and a bombardier was thereby wounded, occasioned by a flaw in the shell, which burst in the mortar," was the day's entry in the official log of the siege.[30]

On May 9, Pepperrell had called on Governor Duchambon to surrender Louisbourg. The General's

---

[30] Pepperrell, William, An Accurate Journal and Account of the Proceedings of New England Land Forces During the Late Expedition Against the French Settlements on Cape Breton to the Time of the Surrender Society of Louisbourg, Massachusetts Historical Society, p. 12-14.

"To The Uttermost Of My Power"

report for the day noted the governor's response. He had declined saying "that the King, his master, having instructed him with the defense of the island, he could not harken to any such proposal, 'til after the most vigorous attack and that he had no answer to make but by the mouth of his cannons."[31]

He was not ready to give up.

The very next day, Duchambon had his men open the gates and attacked several battery sites still under construction. They were quickly repulsed, but the attack showed the French still had plenty of life left in them.

The French also were setting up some batteries of their own on the parapets and at key locations throughout the city. They especially concentrated on covering the harbor area to protect any ships that might break the blockade and make it safely to the city docks. Duchambon had heard reports the French ship *Vigilant* would soon be making an attempt to re-supply the city and he wanted to insure it arrived safely.[32]

On May 9th, the records of the War Council noted the members had agreed to have the Army storm the fortress at night. Parkman says it would have been a futile attack, because as yet there was no breach in the wall and the French were so secure behind Vauban's stoneworks that even women could turn back an attack. Another council meeting that same day voted to rescind the attack due to inopportune conditions. Frustration was growing for everyone.

---

[31] Ibid, p.16.
[32] Leckie, Robert, *The Wars of America*, p. 30-37.

"To The Uttermost Of My Power"

On May 13th, Duchambon had something to cheer about when a sail entered the harbor at Louisbourg and raised a French flag. The ship was a snow -- a large, two-mast merchant ship -- from Bordeaux. Somehow she had escaped the blockade net put out around Louisbourg by Tyng and his colonial cruisers and Warren and his Royal Navy ships.

AT THE SAME TIME, PEPPERRELL'S TROOPS WERE STILL HAVING DIFFICULTY MOVING THE CANNON OVER THE SWAMPY and boggy ground. As their clothing disintegrated as they worked in the mud and the swamps, soldiers became more unruly. No doubt the daily grog ration helped to promote the drunkenness in the camp. Pepperrell had to tread lightly -- these men elected their own officers and he knew the militia could un-elect them too and that would create incredible chaos. Commodore Warren could treat his sailors with normal military discipline; Pepperrell could not with the Army if he wanted to maintain it as a body.

The gun placement problem remained an issue. A battery of six heavy guns was still in place and able to fire shells into the city and against the walls, but more batteries were needed to make the siege truly effective. Luckily, the New England Land Forces included an officer who was able to come up with a solution to that particular problem. He was a New Hampshire Yankee and a neighbor of Pepperrell's in the Piscataqua basin.

Nathaniel Meserve, a lieutenant colonel in a New Hampshire regiment and a boat-builder from Portsmouth, used his ingenuity to develop a wooden sledge that, using 200 men hauling as beasts of burden, could be dragged over swamp, mud, and tidal flats, or almost any obstacle.

"To The Uttermost Of My Power"

Pepperrell reviewed the design and then ordered the sledges built and put to use. It took a full two weeks of tough, dirty work, but by then a 25-gun battery was in place and firing into the city. Additional batteries were being set up all around the fortress. Meserve's sledges were a Godsend.

Pepperrell did not know it at the time, but the sledges actually were doubly successful. Not only did they get the guns into position, the work itself had a major impact on French morale. The defenders were well aware of the problems the Provincials were having and they fervently hoped the marshes and swamps would help defeat the invaders. Once Meserve's sledges began to work and the gun batteries took shape, however, the French realized that yet another of their dwindling hopes for salvation were dashed.

The siege would go on.

On May 19th, the Army was heartened when more ships arrived to add their strength to Warren's squadron. They were *Princess Mary*, 60 guns, and *Hector*, 40 guns, and they immediately joined the blockade.

LATE ON THE SAME DAY, THE SOUND OF GUNFIRE AT SEA alerted Pepperrell that Warren's fleet was in action. The new French ship-of-the-line *Vigilant*, 64 guns, captained by the Comte de la Maisonfort, and carrying almost 600 soldiers to reinforce the garrison, tried to run the blockade, but it was surrounded by too many of Warren's and Tyng's ships. The *Vigilant* had to lower her flag in plain sight of Louisbourg's defenders. Warren found the newly built ship eminently serviceable, and he added it to his blockading fleet.

"To The Uttermost Of My Power"

The taking of the *Vigilant* provided another bonus for the New Englanders. Deep in her cargo hold were barrel after barrel of gunpowder, something rapidly disappearing from the supply depots of Pepperrell's Army. Warren sent a bountiful supply to the men ashore.

Meanwhile, every day more and more cannon and mortars were being dragged to the siege lines. A fifth battery was set up on Martissan Hill, an elevation within range of the city walls. Known as Titcomb's Battery, it had up to five 42-pound cannon taken from the Royal Battery and in time it would wreck havoc on the French. At one point during the construction of this battery, soldiers found 36 cannon of various sizes that the French had dumped into a cove. Before long, they were recovered and joined in the battle line.

By end of the fourth week of the siege, Commodore Warren was getting anxious for conclusive action. Although two additional Royal Navy ships had joined his blockading force, the Commodore still feared the imminent arrival of a superior French fleet. His ships just cruised back and forth in front of the harbor, and he knew at any time a ship bearing new orders from the Admiralty could find him before Louisbourg fell.

Attention now turned to the Island Battery. Warren wanted to attack this isolated gun emplacement and then break into the harbor with his fleet, and he wanted to use most of Pepperrell's men to do it. The eager William Vaughn told Pepperrell he could take the Island Battery as long as he was given total authority to run the operation.

"To The Uttermost Of My Power"

Pepperrell saw these two requests as attempts to usurp his power as commander-in-chief, and he was not going to allow that to happen. He agreed to attack the Island Battery, but he retained overall control of the operation. He also told Warren too many of his soldiers were sick and he could only spare 400 men, which, he felt, should be enough. Pepperrell was firm and stood his ground.

As far as Vaughn was concerned, he would not have led the assault no matter what Pepperrell decided. The militia had spoken, and they elected a new leader to replace Vaughn, a man whom history remembers only as "Captain Brooks."

Warren agreed with the plan to attack the Island Battery. The troops from the Army would all be volunteers and Brooks would lead them. The volunteers gathered at the Royal Battery on the night of the 23rd, but the attack was postponed because the moonlight was too bright. Two nights later, on the 25th, conditions seemed perfect. About 400 men got into boats and began to paddle silently across the harbor to the Island Battery.

General Pepperrell was nervously waiting for news of the attack. In spite of his worries about great loss of life, he had high hopes for success. Earlier, on May 16th, he had written about his optimism to his "tent-maker" in Portsmouth, Governor Benning Wentworth. "I hope that, under God, we shall soon be masters of this island, and that I shall have the pleasure of writing to you from within the walls of Louisbourg."[33]

On the ramparts of the Island Battery, the French sentries paced back and forth, looking in all directions

---

[33] Parsons, Pepperrell to Wentworth, May 16, 1745, p. 79.

"To The Uttermost Of My Power"

but seeing nothing in the gloomy darkness. Down below, men were quietly coming ashore and unloading their boats. Then, for some unknown reason, a soldier in a boat approaching the island broke the silence and gave three cheers to the invaders. As the sounds of that fatal "hip-hip-hooray" faded into the night, they were quickly replaced by the grimmer sounds of muskets firing hot lead and cannon firing muzzles full of grape shot into the huddled mass of New England soldiers. The volleys turned night into day.

About 150 men were ashore, and they were preparing scaling ladders to get over the walls. The French fire was overwhelming and the leader, Brooks, was cut down attempting to climb the wall. The flashes from the French muskets and cannon turned the gloom on the island into near daylight.

Guns roared back and forth for what was an eternity to the men on the island, caught in a terrible, ugly crossfire. Finally as the dawn approached, the Provincials realized the futility of it all. The survivors on the island tried to get back to their boats; some did, many did not. Pepperrell lost 189 men, a little less than half of the force he had contributed to the attack.

The French had their only victory of the campaign, and they celebrated with cheers and cannon fire throughout the next day.

Pepperrell was shocked by the punishment inflicted on his men, but he didn't shirk from his duty. Instead, he responded by setting up another battery, this time on Lighthouse Point, a spit of land with a lighthouse within range of the Island Battery. Colonel Richard Gridley, who thirty years later would arrange the artillery on

"To The Uttermost Of My Power"

Bunker Hill, set up these mortars and cannon as they began to lob shot and shell onto the French fortifications.

And the longer they fired, the more effective they became. Parkman said the fire eventually became so accurate that often French soldiers on the Island Battery could be seen scattering across the terrain to avoid an accurately launched mortar shell.

Shortly after the Island Battery debacle, rumors reached Pepperrell of a French land force coming from Quebec to rescue Louisbourg. This was the French and Indian force of about 700 men led by the partisan Colonel Marin that had been sent to lift the siege of Annapolis Royal. The column had been on Cape Breton Island for some time, and now it was moving on toward Louisbourg.

This threat from the French grabbed the attention of Pepperrell's men, many of whom were having problems staying sober. Pepperrell sent a column of his best troops out after the French force and they soon were driven off the island and back toward Quebec.

Meanwhile, friction had been growing between Pepperrell and Warren. Frustrated by the siege, Warren wanted immediate action taken so he could go on to other things. Pepperrell had only one thing one his mind -- reducing the fortress with as little loss of life as possible. In spite of their cordiality, they seemed to be at lager heads with each other as time went on, as if they were getting close to the breaking point.

1. SIR WILLIAM PEPPERRELL AS COLONEL OF THE 51st REGIMENT

2. THE PEPPERRELL MANSION TODAY
Photograph by Trevor Brayall

3. THE LADY PEPPERRELL HOUSE
Photograph by Trevor Brayall

4. The First Congregational Church
Photograph by Trevor Brayall

5. A brigantine, the work horse of the family fleet

6. KITTERY POINT, MAINE, ROAD SIGN
Photograph by Trevor Brayall

7. THE WHITE BLOCKHOUSE OF FT. MCCLARY OVERLOOKING
PEPPERRELL COVE AND THE PISCATAQUA
Photograph by Trevor Brayall

8. KITTERY POINT FROM KITTERY, LOOKING OVER SPRUCE CREEK
Photograph by Trevor Brayall

9. A RIVER OF BRIDGES
Photograph by Trevor Brayall

"To The Uttermost Of My Power"

Chapter XI

Dissention In Command

COMMODORE WARREN WAS BECOMING IMPATIENT AGAIN.

The fiasco at the Island Battery had ignited his aggressive nature, and he was becoming frustrated with Pepperrell and his amateur Army. To get around Pepperrell and his war board, Warren held a meeting of his captains on the *Superb*. Pepperrell was invited, but Warren was not surprised when he did not appear.

At the meeting, the captains, under Warren's leadership, planned an assault on the fortress and the Island Battery using almost all of Pepperrell's Army. When Warren told him of the plan, Pepperrell diplomatically replied that because of the threatened partisan attack and sickness in the ranks, he couldn't supply the 1,500 men Warren wanted.

Pepperrell felt he could not go along with all the requests without losing control of the Army, and that he absolutely refused to do.

An angry and impatient Warren wrote Pepperrell: "I am very sorry that no plan of mine approved by my captains, has been so fortunate as to meet your approbation or have any weight with you."[34] To further rub his nose in it, Warren sent along a letter from Shirley where the governor expressed his wish that Warren had total command of the expedition.

---

[34] Parkman, Warren to Pepperrell, May 29, 1745, p. 661.

"To The Uttermost Of My Power"

In the face of this, Pepperrell kept his temper in check, noting heavy fog prevented him from attending the council on board ship. He would let Warren vent, but he wouldn't engage in argument. He must have wondered how Navy captains out to sea could even begin to suggest how the Army should conduct a land campaign. That was his job.

Pepperrell did not forget this incident where Warren challenged his command. In a July letter to Governor Shirley after the siege was over, he mentioned the incident to his immediate superior, noting Warren's strong feeling that he, the Commodore, should command the entire mad scheme. "He told me he was the chief officer here," Pepperrell wrote, "but I told him not on shoar (sic)."[35]

Neither man pursued the issue any further and within days it would become a moot point. Both men, in fact, were waiting for several more Royal Navy ships Shirley in Boston had sent north to re-supply the New England Land Forces.

At an informal meeting of his war council, Pepperrell looked for ways to defend the good work his Army had already done. The General took up his pen to do it.

On May 28, Pepperrell sent Warren a lengthy summary of what the Army had accomplished so far during the siege. In addition to landing safely, the General wrote, the Army had built its camp and sanitary facilities; it had driven all the enemy within the walls; it had built five batteries and prepared cannon and mortars to bombard the city continually to the great "distress" of the

---

[35] Parkman, p. 622.

"To The Uttermost Of My Power"

residents; it had taken the Royal Battery and turned the guns there on the fortress; it had made five different assaults on the fortress including the failure at the Island Battery; its scouts have constantly been out to safeguard its position; and Army artillery shelling had already breached the western wall to a significant degree.

In addition, Pepperrell wrote, disease has hit the Army and currently there were only 2,100 soldiers healthy enough for duty. Of that total, 600 had been sent out on expeditions to intercept two groups of French and the Army, he said, "is very much fatigued" because of the nonstop activity.[36]

Not mentioned in Pepperrell's letter, but inherent in nearly every phrase, was the fact this was essentially an amateur Army trying to conquer a professionally built fortress.

By early June, powder and shot were running low, and the firing on Louisbourg eased up as the Army conserved munitions under Pepperrell's order. He was planning a little surprise for the French.

June 11th was the anniversary of King George II's ascension to the throne, and Pepperrell wanted Duchambon to know it. At precisely noon that day, every gun in the siege lines opened up with a massive, simultaneous barrage of cannonballs and grapeshot that shattered the noonday silence. And the firing didn't stop, but rather volley after volley battered the French

---

[36] Parsons, Pepperrell to Warren, May 28, 1745, p. 82.

"To The Uttermost Of My Power"

lines, "which much disheartened the enemy,"[37] according to Pepperrell's official report.

The very next day, the report continued, *Canterbury* and *Sunderland* joined the fleet with their long-awaited supplies. "Accordingly . . . the transports were ordered off, to take out the spare masts, yards and other lumber of the men-of-war. The soldiers were imployed in getting moss to barricade their nettings, and 600 men were sent about the Kings ships at the commodore's request."[38]

A new, larger mortar was added to the Lighthouse Battery, which finally was beginning to silence the Island Battery. Titcomb's Battery also was reinforced and it continued effectively destroying the stonewall that surrounded the city.

Being re-supplied with new powder and provisions, Pepperrell agreed with Warren to make a full attack on the remains of the fortress on the first good day after the ships' arrival. Preparations were well under way for the big push that should result in the fall of the fortress of Louisbourg.

Warren remained eager for combat even as his fleet grew in size and power. His Royal Navy Squadron now included the following vessels: *Superb*, flagship, 60 guns; *Princess Mary*, 60; *Sunderland*, 60; *Canterbury*, 60; *Chester*, 50: *Eltham*, 40; *Mermaid*, 40; *Launceton*, 40; *Hector*, 40; and *Lark*, 30. Captured French ships, which in general were better built than British ones, *Vigilant*,

---

[37] Pepperrell, *Authentic Report*.
[38] Ibid.

"To The Uttermost Of My Power"

60 and *Bon Amie*, 30, now sailed under the Union Jack.[39]

Pepperrell was moving slowly, and that was the way he wanted it for right now. Supplies had been restocked, more powder had been unloaded and the Army had more cannons to turn into batteries.

The Lieutenant General from Kittery had agreed with Warren that there was a need for another attack. It would let Warren get his ships in the harbor, and should give New England the Island Battery, and would give them the town. But at what cost, Pepperrell wondered.

Warren, for example, could coldly order his ships to go anywhere he wanted them to go and when, and there was nothing short of mutiny his men could do about it. That was their tradition and their job. But the New England Army was not an army of strangers. These people had faces -- a lot of those people were his friends from Kittery, Portsmouth, Boston and from throughout New England. Pepperrell knew it was difficult to order a wholesale assault when you were sending your friends to their death.

Pepperrell intended to strengthen the siege with more guns in more batteries, firing more often to break down the walls and render Louisbourg helpless. All it would take is more time, he thought.

Pepperrell was not making these decisions in a vacuum. His subordinate staff, Major General Wolcott and

---

[39] Deforest, *Louisbourg Journals*, p. 181.

"To The Uttermost Of My Power"

Brigadier Generals Dwight and Waldo, were in accord with their commander. Waldo, in fact, warned his old friend not to do anything to set off Warren's famous temper. Pepperrell told Waldo everything was under control.

The way into Louisbourg, Pepperrell knew, lay in increasing the artillery barrage and pounding the fortress into submission. That was still his plan. But he still had to deal with Warren and his desire for a strong central attack. Pepperrell and his men prepared for it.

BUT IT WOULD NEVER COME.

The War Council, including Commodore Warren, set the assault for June 15. But fate apparently had other things in mind that day. Captain Joseph Sherburn, a New England artillery officer, wrote in his diary: "By 12 o'clock, we had got all our platforms laid, embrasures mended, guns in order, shot in place, cartridges ready, dined, gunners quartered, matches lighted to return their favors, when we heard their drums beat a parley; soon there appeared a flag of truce, which we received midway between our battery and their walls." [40]

A native of Portsmouth, Sherburn came to Louisbourg as a sergeant in Colonel Samuel Moore's New Hampshire regiment. On May 17, however, General Pepperrell promoted the 51-year-old veteran to command one of two newly built batteries near the city's main gate. It made him the first New England officer in position to see the white flag flown by the French and to receive the emissary. Sherburn and his command cheered as the French representatives passed through their lines.

---

[40] Leckie, *Wars* p. 37.

"To The Uttermost Of My Power"

The French had had enough.

Victory, a nearly impossible, incredible victory, was at hand.

"To The Uttermost Of My Power"

Chapter XII

"The Happy Issue"

AS THE NEW ENGLANDERS PREPARED FOR THEIR NEXT ACTION, THE FRENCH INHABITANTS OF LOUISBOURG WERE TAKING SOME ACTION OF THEIR OWN.

After meeting privately and discussing options, leaders of the citizens went directly to Governor Duchambon with a petition demanding he surrender the fortress. Any popular support the governor had retained, vanished in the crushing artillery fire.

While Governor Duchambon remained combative, he nonetheless asked his chief engineer to survey the situation and report back quickly. When the report was received, Duchambon found he really had no choice. The report said the city's defensive walls were crumbling, there was no hope of rescue or re-supply, morale did not exist, and they were slowly starving. Very few of the houses in the town were undamaged. It was also easy to see the "Bastonais" were preparing another attack. The French council debated briefly, then voted.

"All of the houses in the town were demolished, full of holes and uninhabitable," the embattled French governor wrote. The council decided unanimously to capitulate, Duchambon told the French ministry of war in his report.

At noon on June 15, Captain Sherburn's troops in the front line noticed a white flag fluttering over the battlements. A cheer went up and word was quickly

"To The Uttermost Of My Power"

passed to Pepperrell's headquarters that the French apparently wanted to talk.

Lt. General Pepperrell and Commodore Warren happened to be at the Green Hill Battery site, and they conferred quickly -- perhaps in Benning Wentworth's tent. They decided to give Duchambon until eight o'clock the next morning to propose his terms for surrender and the word was passed back to the French lines.

There would be no final attack.

When Duchambon sent his proposed terms for surrender through the lines the next morning, Pepperrell rejected them immediately. The French proposed too many conditions, most of which dealt with military protocol. The New Englanders were more in the mood for unconditional surrender. Pepperrell sent his own terms back to Duchambon, who had the choice of accepting them or continuing to fight. Duchambon then found Pepperrell's terms acceptable, and the French finally raised the white flag of surrender over Louisbourg.

Basically, Pepperrell demanded the parole of the garrison, meaning they could not bear arms against England for the duration of the war. The garrison was allowed to parade from the fortress with their own colors before boarding ships for France. The residents of Louisbourg were promised protection of their lives and property -- which meant no plunder for the Provincials. They also had the choice of leaving with the garrison.

Louisbourg would be surrendered the next morning, exactly seven weeks from the day the siege began. It was nothing less than a miracle.

"To The Uttermost Of My Power"

General Pepperrell didn't know it at the time, but he had made a mistake in surrender protocol and procedure. The mistake was made out of ignorance and not intent. Warren drew his attention to the mistake. "It is not regular, you will please to observe, to do it (receive the surrender) till all the articles are ratified by both sides, which I will hasten to get done in time." It was. Warren understood the General's inexperience and never held the transgression against Pepperrell.

On June 16, 1745, the New England Provincial soldiers lined up to watch the defeated Gallic Army leave. With trumpets blaring and flags waving, the French garrison marched out with flags flying and then laid down their arms. They set up a camp outside the city walls. By July 15, they were gone.

Pepperrell himself met Duchambon at the South Gate, where the former governor handed the keys to the fortress to the Kittery merchant-turned-conqueror. Following that ceremony -- Warren himself was eager to get the keys and take more credit for the victory than he deserved, but he was busy accepting the surrender of the Island Battery -- the New England Land Forces moved into the city to protect the very people and houses they had come to plunder.

Watching his Army move into the city, Pepperrell knew his main problem was going to be the prevention of looting in the city. While many of the houses were in ruins, enough remained in the city to tempt his men. To counter the natural avarice of the fighting man, Pepperrell issued orders for the men to behave and keep their hands off things that didn't belong to them. He vowed punishment for violators, thinking the sight of

"To The Uttermost Of My Power"

looters receiving a hundred lashes would certainly be a deterrent.

Although the Army couldn't, the Navy was able to profit quite nicely from the surrender and do it legally. Warren knew that French ships were in the vicinity, so he pulled most of his warships into the harbor and well out of view. Then he ordered the French flags flown from the Island Battery and the King's Bastion, both locations clearly visible from the sea. Thinking their country men still controlled Louisbourg and with no English sail in sight, ship after ship made its way into the harbor where they were caught in Warren's trap. All told, seven ships and their cargo were now prizes of war for the Navy, with a total value of one million dollars.

Then, to the amazement of even Warren, the French frigate *Notre Dame de la deliverance* sailed into the harbor and was snared. A detailed search of the ship found almost four million dollars in silver ore and silver coin.

Though some people thought of this as piracy, the taking of prizes by the Navy was an age-old custom designed to compensate the often-overworked sailors. Warren's share would total some sixty thousand pounds, making him a very rich man.

Pepperrell and his men made no such money on the siege. He attempted to complain about this inequity when he wrote to the Duke of Newcastle the ships were captured in plain sight of the Army and might that not

"To The Uttermost Of My Power"

be cause to share the prize money? The Duke deigned not to answer the question.[41]

Pepperrell cared nothing for prize money for himself, but he felt his men had earned something for all they had done to besiege Louisbourg. It was the Army that fought the French on the Island Battery; it was the Army that had dragged artillery across fields of mud; it was the Army that slept on wet ground and had suffered under the return fire from the fortress. The Navy, while playing a vital role in the victory, had slept in their warm hammocks every night, and they rarely, if ever, had to face dangerous fire. The General protested to anyone who would listen, but to no avail.

Pepperrell had already contributed a substantial amount of his own money to help besiege Louisbourg, estimated at nearly 10,000 pounds. To commemorate and celebrate the victory, he would spend even more to host a large banquet for key Army and Navy officers who had helped to make victory possible.

As the guests prepared to dine, Pepperrell called on his wife's uncle, Rev. Samuel Moody, to give the blessing and benediction. Now many of the diners feared Moody -- not known for brevity -- would talk so long the food would be cold.

"Good Lord, we have so much to thank thee for, that time will be too short, and that we must leave it for eternity," Moody intoned. "God bless our food and fellowship upon this joyful occasion for the sake of our

---

[41] Parsons, Pepperrell to Newcastle, October 3, 1745, p. 127-128.

"To The Uttermost Of My Power"

Lord." Then he sat down, ready to eat. Hunger had conquered verbosity.[42]

ONE OF THE VERY FIRST THINGS PEPPERRELL DID ONCE HE KNEW THE FRENCH were surrendering was to send a very fast ship back to Boston to bring the good news to Governor Shirley. The military frigate arrived in Boston at 1 AM on July 4th, but Captain Moses Bennett didn't wait for the sun to come up to spread the news. He went directly to Shirley's mansion in Roxbury and woke him up in the middle of the night with the joyous information.

By midmorning on July 4th, the entire town of Boston knew Pepperrell and the New England Land Forces had eliminated the threat of Louisbourg. Cannon fired and church bells rang in celebration all day long. An elated Gov. Shirley declared the following Thursday to be a day of thanksgiving in the colony.

In his report to Shirley, Pepperrell wrote:

> May it please your Excellency, it is with the greatest pleasure that I give you and my country on the happy issue of our enterprise against Louisbourg, which was through God's goodness by the surrender of the fortress etc., on the 16th instant. Upon the terms of capitulation agreed to with the governor of said place, by Commodore Warren and myself, a copy of which I have included to your Excellency, and accordingly the fleet came into the harbor, and a detachment of our troops with myself entered the town estuary . . . The French troops were marched out and embarked aboard ships.[43]

---

[42] Parsons, p. 104.
[43] Parsons, Pepperrell Victory Report to Shirley, p. 104-106.

"To The Uttermost Of My Power"

They had done it; the Bastonais had done the impossible. To make sure London knew who did it, Pepperrell sent a copy of his report and the surrender terms to the Duke of Newcastle in London.

Pepperrell did not forget to tell the Duke and the Governor about the human cost of Louisbourg. In his report, he wrote: "During the whole siege we had no more than one hundred and one men killed by the enemy and all other accidents; no more than 30 died by sickness. According to the best accounts, there were killed of the enemy within the walls alone three hundred besides numbers that died by being confined in the hospital."[44]

The New England Land Forces also captured a wide variety of military stores and equipment. The cache included the ships ensnarled by Warren, as well as 76 cannon and mortars of various sizes and distance range. In addition, nearly 2,500 soldiers and militia men were captured and given their parole after swearing to not bear arms against Britain or the colonies in this war.[45]

A grateful Shirley was able to write back to Pepperrell at Louisbourg on July 7. "I congratulate you and the other officers and the whole army under your command who by their late bravery and unparallell'd services before Louisboug have lay'd a lasting foundation for the wealth, peace and prosperity of this country."[46] He, like everyone else, found it incredible that Pepperrell and his men had done the job in just 49 days -- a mere seven weeks.

---

[44] Ibid.
[45] Parsons, p. 103.
[46] Shirley to Pepperrell, July 7 1745, Miscellaneous Collections, Massachusetts Historical Society.

"To The Uttermost Of My Power"

The town of Boston was not the only center of celebrations. Church bells rang all day long in rural New England. To the south, people in New York and Philadelphia rejoiced with the news, as did residents in other New England communities. Citizens of London and other major English cities celebrated for their American cousins when the news crossed the Atlantic.

The French reacted with consternation when they learned the results of the siege. They had just defeated the English at the Battle of Fontenoy[47] and their armies were racking up victory after victory in Flanders. How could they have lost to an army made up of Provincials? What was this world coming to?

The French intellectual and leader of the Enlightenment, Voltaire, understood the significance of the fall of Louisbourg, calling its conquest by the New England Land Forces the most remarkable thing that happened during the reign of Louis XV.

In the moment of victory, Pepperrell was generous with praise in his report to Shirley. "I need not express again to you Sir, that I esteem it of the happiest consequence that his majesty's ships were sent here under the command of a gentleman whose distinguished merit and goodness New England claims a particular right to honor and rejoice in," Pepperrell told Shirley, paying the

---

[47] On May 11, 1745, French forces clashed with an Austrian-British Army led by the Duke of Cumberland, George II's youngest son at the field of Fontenoy in Belgium. The French thoroughly trounced the allied Army in one of the largest battles of The War of The Austrian Succession.

"To The Uttermost Of My Power"

highest compliments to Commodore Warren in spite of their differences during the siege.[48]

Pepperrell himself received lavish praise for reducing the great fortress in less than two months. Rev. Charles Chauncey wrote to his brother-in-law "as God has made you an instrument of so much service to your country the hazard of your life and the expense of great labor and fatigue, your name is deservedly and universally spoken of with respect and I doubt not that you will be handed down with honor for the latest posterity."[49]

Indeed, Pepperrell received hundreds of congratulatory letters from all over the colonies and England. He was lauded as a true hero, a Cincinatus of New England, who, having defeated the enemy would return to his plow -- or in this case his counting house.

He was the most famous man in New England, and perhaps for a brief moment in time, the most famous in the English-speaking world.

However, some reaction in England itself was more restrained. After all, the scope of battle at Louisbourg was much smaller than most contests fought in Europe. The Provincial force only numbered 4,500 men and the French garrison was even smaller. Coming on the heels of the defeat by the French at Fontenoy and the landing of "Bonnie Prince Charlie" Stuart in Scotland prior to the

---

[48] Pepperrell, *Authentic Report.*
[49] Parsons, Chauncey to Pepperrell, July 4, 1745, p. 108.

"To The Uttermost Of My Power"

Battle of Culloden,[50] Louisbourg seemed like a minor skirmish.

But was there another reason for the restrained reaction? Maybe some members of Parliament could see into the future.

In many ways, the seeds for Lexington and Concord were sown at Louisbourg. The inter-colonial effort showed the New England colonies they could work together to obtain a military victory. Colonial leaders now knew they could develop and train a fighting force to protect their own interests without help from London.

The expedition also demonstrated to the soldiers who fought that they were as good as anyone else in battle, even though they didn't face first-class European troops at Louisbourg. But when the moment came to fire at Bunker Hill, the Patriots proved they had learned their lessons well on Cape Breton Island.

Some of the men who fought at Louisbourg with Pepperrell were to make their mark years later when the colonies made their united move for independence. For example, Major Seth Pomeroy was a gunner from Northampton, Massachusetts, who fought at Louisbourg.

---

[50] Charles Edward Stuart was the grandson of King James II, and pretender for the crown James wore until the Glorious Revolution of 1688 ended with his removal from the throne. Supported by the French as well as Scottish and Irish rebels, Prince Charlie and his army landed in Scotland in July of 1745. After defeating a local army and capturing Edinburgh, he was caught by a British force led by the Duke of Cumberland, the younger son of King George II and the commander in chief of the British Army, at the Battle of Culloden in April 1746. The Stuart Army was destroyed and he fled to Europe. That defeat was the last gasp of the Jacobite party that sought the restoration -- for a second time -- of the Stuarts.

"To The Uttermost Of My Power"

Ten years later, he fought unsuccessfully with a British and colonial force to defend Fort William Henry from the French at Lake George, New York. Two decades beyond that, Pomeroy was on the Patriot side, facing the redcoat charge at Bunker Hill. And the man who set up the cannon on that hill in Charlestown, Massachusetts, in 1775 was Richard Gridley, Pepperrell's chief of artillery at Louisbourg.

There were others in that New England Army who went on to serve in the Revolution.

John Nixon of Framingham, Massachusetts, was a soldier at Louisbourg, and he became a brigadier general in the Continental Army. Captain David Wooster of the Connecticut militia became a major general of state troops during the Revolution, serving until he was killed in action. Matthew Thornton of New Hampshire served as a surgeon with one of the colony's regiments at Louisbourg; in 1776, Thornton signed the Declaration of Independence. Also signing that "traitorous" document was Oliver Wolcott, son of Pepperrell's second-in-command at Louisbourg, Roger Wolcott of Connecticut.

Meanwhile, the Duke of Newcastle wrote the following to Pepperrell:

> I have the pleasure to acquaint you that the news of the reduction of Louisbourg was received by his Majesty with the highest satisfaction, which the King has commanded should be signified to all the commanders and other officers, both land and sea who were instrumental therein; in consequence of which, I am to desire you would acquaint the officers under your command with his Majesty's most gracious approbation of their services upon this occasion.

"To The Uttermost Of My Power"

Newcastle continued: "It is a great satisfaction to me to acquaint you that his Majesty has thought fit to distinguish the commander-in-chief of this expedition, by conferring on you the dignity of a Baronet of Great Britain (upon which I beg leave to most sincerely congratulate you) and to give a flag to Commodore Warren (make him an admiral)."[51]

Pepperrell was amazed by the honor he was given, and he was very happy about Warren's promotion. The Royal Navy in those days of fighting sail had three divisions, the blue, the white and the red. When an officer received flag rank, he became rear admiral of the blue. His next promotion would be to rear admiral of the white, then rear admiral of the red. Then he would become vice admiral of the blue, white and red successively. Next would come admiral of the blue and then white. The post of admiral of the red was usually held vacant. Promotion through the admiral's rankings took a long time. The legendary Horatio Nelson was only a vice admiral of the white at his death during the Battle of Trafalgar in 1805. If an officer became an admiral and had no command, he was left ashore at half pay as an admiral of the yellow.

In addition to those major honors, both Pepperrell and Governor Shirley were given the authority to recruit troops from the colonies to form their own regiments in the British Army. Shirley's was the 50th Regiment of Foot while Pepperrell's was the 51st Regiment of Foot. The men became the "colonels" commanding the regiments, although they did not have to serve. This honor earned the honoree between three and four thousand pounds per year in revenue.

---

[51] Parsons, Newcastle to Pepperrell, August 10, 1745,

"To The Uttermost Of My Power"

Shirley, the great promoter of Louisbourg, was upset because he did not get a baronetcy. He certainly resented Pepperrell's good fortune, but the Kittery man never sought the honor; the abrasive Shirley did. The Governor was even more upset several years later when Admiral Warren became a baronet.

There is little doubt, however, that if Pepperrell deserved a baronetcy for leading the expedition, Shirley probably deserved one for organizing and managing the logistics for it.[52] But it is also true that field commanders win the accolades and rewards, not the planners and suppliers.

These two men of Massachusetts -- Shirley from London and Pepperrell from Maine -- were definitely a study in contrasts. Shirley was European, born in London; Pepperrell was an American, born in Kittery. Shirley was eager and combative; Pepperrell was solid and honest. Shirley devised the strategy at Louisbourg; Pepperrell was the battlefield leader who carried it out. Shirley was incredibly ambitious and he would do anything to get ahead; Pepperrell was a calming influence and waited for good things to come to him. Shirley was the promoter of the mad scheme, but Pepperrell certainly was the man who made it work.

In truth, they were both true heroes of Louisbourg. One could not have succeeded without the other.

Nathaniel Hawthorne, in his sketch of Pepperrell, gave this assessment of the men of Louisbourg.

---

[52] Warren also was offered a baronetcy, but he turned it down because he had no children to inherit the title. He later accepted the honor, not for Louisbourg, but for valor in naval combat with the French.

"To The Uttermost Of My Power"

> The arms of Great Britain were not crowned by a more brilliant achievement during that unprosperous war; and, in adjusting the terms of a subsequent peace, Louisburg was an equivalent for many losses nearer home. The English, with very pardonable vanity, attributed the conquest chiefly to the valor of the naval force. On the Continent of Europe, our fathers met with greater justice...Shirley, originally a lawyer, was commissioned in the regular Army, and rose to the supreme military command in America. Warren, also, received honors and professional rank, and arrogated to him, without scruple, the whole crop of laurels gathered at Louisbourg. Pepperrell was placed at the head of a royal regiment, and, first of his countrymen, was distinguished by the title of baronet.[53]

Whatever the outcome, whatever people thought, Pepperrell had done his job, had achieved the impossible. Somehow he had taken a rag-tag bunch of farmers and sailors and turned them into an army long enough for them to conquer and occupy the strongest, most modern fortress in the Americas.

MANY MODERN WRITERS AND HISTORIANS WHO HAVE LOOKED INTO THE FIRST SIEGE OF LOUISBOURG HAVE come to the conclusion the victory there was the result of some sort of good luck bestowed on a bunch of amateurs by the various gods of war. In reality, there was little luck at Louisbourg, with the exception of the capture of the Royal Battery. The success achieved by Pepperrell's Army happened because Pepperrell and his staff conducted their operations in a professional manner, sought the safest way to do things, and strove to lose as few men as possible. It may have been an amateur plan carried out by amateurs, but the result was a professional surrender by a professional garrison to what had become a professional army besieging it.

---

[53] Hawthorne.

"TO THE UTTERMOST OF MY POWER"

Pepperrell had stood his ground against Governor Shirley -- and Commodore Warren -- to do what he felt was the right thing to do at Louisbourg. Based on the results, he was correct.

"To The Uttermost Of My Power"

Chapter XIII

"To The Uttermost . . ."

IF THE VICTORY AT LOUISBOURG WAS THE HIGH POINT OF WILLIAM PEPPERRELL'S LIFE, THE NEXT YEAR OF THE OCCUPATION OF THE CONQUERED FRENCH STRONGHOLD CERTAINLY WAS THE LOW POINT.

After winning the victory over the French, the men of New England discovered they would be an occupying force and they couldn't go home. They were not happy.

In June and July, the air was heady with the feeling of victory at Louisbourg. The French had marched out of the fortress the day after their surrender. They put down their arms, furled their battle flags and marched down to the ships that would take them back to France, where they would serve their parole.

Except for a few residents, the city, fortress, and the surrounding Cape Breton Island were all in the hands of the New England Land Forces now. Managing it was going to be the problem.

The problem with Louisbourg was one that tormented everyone who had ever served there since the fortress was built -- the glaring, terrifying boredom of the place. There was literally nothing to do. There were no taverns or places to get drunk, so the colonial troops normally went out into the woods. They had had plenty of practice during the siege.

"TO THE UTTERMOST OF MY POWER"

In addition, the weather changed again. During the siege, it had been fairly mild, but after the French surrender, it became rainy, miserable and cold. Clothing disintegrated due to the weather, the ground became a sea of mud, and it was just plain miserable for all. The troops could not even take refuge in the houses of Louisbourg because their siege artillery had done such a good job of destroying them. They were unlivable.

To combat these situations affecting the sailors, Warren had the advantage of sending his men somewhere with their ships and at least having them be out to sea. Pepperrell's men had only the land, and that was pure misery.

Another ages-old problem afflicted the New England Army -- women, more specifically the lack thereof. The men had been away from home for several months, and they were getting lonely and eager for female companionship. The Army had its traditional camp followers, but most of them were wives of non-commissioned officers, sergeants and private soldiers who accompanied their husbands to war. Most were not prostitutes; rather they did laundry and cooked meals. The French inhabitants had left and taken their wives and daughters with them. The pious Pepperrell would not import women or encourage their venturing to Louisbourg. There seemed to be no solution to this problem, and it was just another burning fuse for Pepperrell to watch.

Pepperrell later said he spent half of his waking hours after the fall of Louisbourg handling courts-martial for his recalcitrant men, and Warren spent a lot of his time handling legal and punishment matters as well. Apparently the makeshift jails on land were heavily

"To The Uttermost Of My Power"

populated throughout the Army's stay at Louisbourg, and the floating jails of the Navy -- the brigs -- were full much of the time as well.

Pepperrell and Warren agreed the fortress needed to be occupied at least until Britain sent regular troops over to garrison Louisbourg, or they decided to destroy it. The two commanders wrote a joint letter to the Duke of Newcastle shortly after the victory in which they advocated the establishment of a civil government, replete with garrison and governor.

In an ambitious twist, Pepperrell put in his bid for the latter post in the July 30th letter. He wrote: "My Lord Duke, I beg leave to trouble yr. Grace to request yr. Favor on my behalf to His Majesty, that if my services in ye expedition against this place have merit'd his Majesty's generous notice, I may obtain His Royal Commission for ye governorship herefor."[54]

The Duke's reply was not contained in his next return letter, which outlined some honors for the two men -- the admiral's flag and the baronetcy. The Duke also told them two regiments were being sent from the Gibraltar fortress to form the garrison at Louisbourg, but His Lordship gave no indication when they would arrive.

PEPPERRELL AND WARREN WERE IN LIMBO OVER THEIR FUTURE PLANS. They both assumed a governor would be coming out from England, and perhaps also a new military commander. Pepperrell had already told the Duke of Newcastle that, having been the commander previously, he would not mind continuing in the post, but he would prefer not to serve under a different officer.

---

[54] Parsons, Pepperrell to Newcastle, July 8, 1745, p. 109.

"To The Uttermost Of My Power"

The Duke's next letter answered the question about the governorship of Cape Breton Island -- the job went to Rear Admiral Peter Warren, while Pepperrell retained command of the New England Land Forces making up the garrison. Ever even-tempered, the new Baronet swallowed any disappointment he might have felt and congratulated the new admiral and governor.

Once the news of Pepperrell's reward became public, the backbiters at home surfaced. Pepperrell's old rival in Portsmouth, Benning Wentworth, claimed the General had over-used, underpaid and generally mistreated the New Hampshire troops in particular. The charge was quietly dropped when soldiers involved said there was no validity to the claims.

Rumors started at Louisbourg and spread to New England that the keys to the fortress were given to Warren and not Pepperrell, who should have received them as the ranking officer on the scene. The General refuted the charge by producing the keys and giving them to Shirley when he visited Louisbourg later in the year. Duchambon had given them to Pepperrell when the French left the ramparts.

Another tale spread throughout New England was the fact Warren signed the surrender document first, taking precedence over Pepperrell. A look at the document proved otherwise.

It almost seemed like a jealous William Shirley was trying to drive a wedge between Pepperrell and Warren with question after question about their relationship. But the new Baronet would not let it happen. Pepperrell constantly kept the record -- and Governor Shirley --

"To The Uttermost Of My Power"

straight, and he was always ready to defend his record and Warren's as well.

Jealousy of Pepperrell seemed in some ways to consume Shirley. He wrote a long letter and a report to the Duke of Newcastle in which he praised Warren, Vaughn, Gridley, Waldo and other officers, but barely mentioned Sir William. It seemed a petty way to treat a man who contributed so much to victory.

Usher Parsons wrote about this, noting "it is doubtful if a parallel can be found where a commander-in-chief, as Shirley was, treated the executive officer, after a successful siege or battle, so indifferently."[55]

Samuel Waldo warned his old friend Shirley was stabbing him in the back, but Pepperrell wouldn't believe him. It would take another decade before Sir William would finally, irrevocably break with Shirley.

It also took a while for the friction between Pepperrell and Warren to die down, but they were totally different men with differing temperaments. Warren was European; Pepperrell was American. Warren was Navy, used to quick action; Pepperrell was Army, used to slow movement. Warren was in charge of a moving blockade; Pepperrell was trying to conduct a siege of a strong fortification. Warren was a military man; Pepperrell was a merchant. Warren was in his 40's; Pepperrell was in his 50's. Warren obeyed direct orders; Pepperrell was used to working with the governor's council in Massachusetts and reaching a consensus. Warren was an autocrat on his ships; Pepperrell the aristocrat was

---

[55] Parsons, p. 295.

"To The Uttermost Of My Power"

more of a democrat because he had to respect the opinion of the militia.

But with time and patience, they did overcome these differences and formed a remarkable and effective partnership between two men who truly liked each other. They remained friends until the end of their lives.

Historian Francis Parkman noted this relationship. "Warren no doubt thought he had a right to precedence, as being an officer of the King in regular standing, while Pepperrell was but a civilian, clothed in temporary rank by the appointment of a provincial governor . . . He (Pepperrell) liked Warren, and to the last continued to praise him highly in letters to Shirley and other provincial governors, while, Warren, on the occasion of Shirley's arrival in Louisbourg, made a speech highly complimentary to both the General and his soldiers."[56]

Writing to Admiral George Anson, who from 1740 to 1743 led a Royal Navy expedition circumnavigating the earth and who was now the First Sea Lord, Warren told Anson to ignore any reports coming out of Massachusetts mentioning a negative relationship. He warned of people in the colony trying to cause trouble, people who "bend . . . to make a breach between the General and me . . . I resented this treatment so warmly that I have had many letters of excuse from numbers of the people concerne'd in the address."[57]

Meanwhile, troop morale for those still at Louisbourg was deteriorating rapidly as summer turned to fall. Some regiments and formations had gone home, as did

---

[56] Parkman, p. 669.
[57] McLennan, J.S., Warren to Anson, p. 178.

"To The Uttermost Of My Power"

Major General Roger Wolcott, the lieutenant governor of Connecticut and Pepperrell's second in command.

After Wolcott was back home in Connecticut, Pepperrell wrote a long, thoughtful letter to him focusing on their lot at Louisbourg and on Pepperrell's faith in the Almighty. "I must say," Pepperrell wrote on December 10, 1745, "that this campaign has borne much upon my constitution and almost wore me out. But if it should please Him who made us willing to come on this expedition to call upon us for some other reason, He can support and carry us through. And I hope that we shall at all times be able to put our trust in him."

Then Pepperrell showed Wolcott just what a kindly man he was as he characterized their official and their interpersonal relationship. It could have been difficult; after all, Wolcott had taken the major general's position from Pepperrell's old friend Samuel Waldo; and he had proven to be slow and ineffectual as a commander. The commanding general, however, could find nothing negative to say about his service at Louisbourg.

"The short acquaintance I had with you sufficed to give me a profound respect and esteem for you, and I should have been glad if your health if had permitted you to remain here longer with us." Pepperrell told Wolcott he hoped he would make a visit to Louisbourg some time in the future -- he never did. But the pair remained friends for the remainder of their days.[58]

The remaining New England troops wanted to go home too -- after all they hadn't volunteered for garrison duty. But they had to wait for those two regiments from

---

[58] Parsons, Pepperrell to Wolcott, August 19, 1746, p. 151.

"To The Uttermost Of My Power"

Gibraltar the Duke of Newcastle had promised. And in every way possible, they blamed Sir William as the one who wouldn't let them go home.

Meanwhile, Shirley bombarded Pepperrell with questions about the siege, the occupation and anything else under the sun. In order to have questions answered quickly, Pepperrell invited Governor Shirley to come to Louisbourg and see the situation for himself.

Shirley and his entourage arrived there on board the *Hector* on August 17th, accompanied by -- to the surprise of all -- Susannah Warren, the New York-born wife of the Admiral. Mary Pepperrell had been invited by Shirley to accompany them as well, but she had declined. She still was not feeling well, and did not like the idea of a sea voyage. As she told her husband the General, she would stay at home and keep sending him clean shirts and tea.

Although the troops were unhappy, they greeted Shirley cordially at first; by September, they were in a mutinous mood and actually planned for one on the 18th. Word of this got back to Pepperrell, Warren and Shirley, and they took action to nip the mutiny in the bud. In doing so, Shirley promised to increase their basic pay from 25 to 40 shillings per month.

By November, Shirley was gone, leaving Pepperrell to manage the remains of the New England Land Forces as best he could.

In spite of all of the unpleasantness of the occupation, Pepperrell never forgot the importance of his duty at Louisbourg. The New Englanders were impatiently awaiting the arrival of those two regiments from Gibraltar that Newcastle had promised so they could go

"To The Uttermost Of My Power"

home. But the New Englanders would defend Louisbourg to the end if the situation arose.

In a November 4th, 1745 letter to his friend Captain Henry Stafford in Exmouth, England, Pepperrell wrote about the family and financial problems that threatened many of the volunteer officers and men. But, he insisted, nothing would deter the Army from doing its duty and protecting the fortress and the city from future attack.

"I resolve," he wrote Stafford "to tarry here and defend it to the uttermost of my power."[59]

As cold weather settled on Louisbourg, so did fever and disease. In October, one-third of the 2,000-man garrison was on the sick list. Warren himself fell ill during this time, but he recovered. In his own turn, Pepperrell contracted several fevers, which weakened his physical condition.

All in all, Pepperrell must have been totally miserable. He was walking a thin line in trying to maintain military discipline and still respect the wishes of the militia. He must have been an incredibly patient man. And he wanted to go home as much as his men did.

He missed his wife.

He worried about his business.

---

[59] Pepperrell to Stafford, November 4, 1745, Miscellaneous Collections, Massachusetts Historical Society.

"To The Uttermost Of My Power"

His son-in-law, Nathaniel Sparhawk, kept pestering him with letters asking him to obtain trade goods from Louisbourg at plunder prices.

He grew tired of defending his actions even though he was able to refute any and all charges against him.

No doubt he was tired of seeing his men, for whom he truly had great affection, die in the boredom that was Louisbourg.

In truth, Pepperrell was almost like a lightning rod for all the bad things related to the expedition to Louisbourg. If your son went to Louisbourg and was killed, it was all Pepperrell's fault; if you got bored, got drunk, got caught and got thrown in the brig, it wasn't your fault, it was Pepperrell's; if your son got sick at Louisbourg, it wasn't his fault, it was Pepperrell's; if you wanted to go home and couldn't, it wasn't your fault, it was Pepperrell's fault; every thing was his fault.

Things got so bad back in New England rumors began to spread saying the Baronet would not be invited back for a new term on the Massachusetts Governor's Council. That didn't happen, but in an election soon after these problems cropped up, Pepperrell's son-in-law, Nathaniel Sparhawk, was defeated in his bid for re-election for a third term representing Kittery as a member of the Great and General Court in Boston. His defeat was blamed on the General's current unpopularity.

It seems Pepperrell might have been partially to blame for Sparhawk's electoral defeat, however. Early in the occupation, Pepperrell and Warren awarded contracts for food and other supplies for the Army at Louisbourg. A large part of those lucrative awards went to the firm of

"To The Uttermost Of My Power"

Sparhawk & Colman, to the anger of the losing bidders, who may have had their revenge at the ballot box.

The death of any one of his soldiers through fighting or disease bothered the General greatly. Undoubtedly, he felt he spent too much time attending funerals for his men. But one death at Louisbourg affected him enormously. His personal physician and close friend, Dr. Alexander Bulman, had been trying to get permission to go home to York, Maine, for quite some time. Finally, he got approval, but before he could leave, the fever got him. He suffered for several days, burning in the damp atmosphere. The medical services there were not enough; he couldn't recover and he died, to Pepperrell's great regret.

An unknown diarist from New England also noted the good doctor's passing on October 12th. "This day died Dr. Alexander Bulman. I believe a Truly Godly and Pious man (Chief Chirurgeon to the General's regiment)," wrote the soldier who is believed to have been from Massachusetts. "He has been Very Serviceable to us and therefore is a great loss, and not only to us but to the town of York to which he belonged."[60]

Louisbourg truly was a double-edged sword for the Army from New England that had attacked it. Nathaniel Hawthorne saw the impact of Louisbourg on colonial society in three ways. First, he wrote, "Most of the young men who had left their paternal firesides, sound in constitution, and pure in morals, if they returned at all, returned with ruined health, and with minds so broken up by the interval of riot, that they never after could resume the habits of good citizenship."

---

[60] DeForest, L.E., *Louisbourg Journals*, p. 42.

"To The Uttermost Of My Power"

In addition, "a lust for military glory was also awakened in the country; and France and England gratified it with enough of slaughter; the former seeking to recover what she had lost, the latter to complete the conquest which the colonists had begun."

Finally, he noted, "Through all this troubled time, the flower of the youth were cut down by the sword, or died of physical diseases, or became unprofitable citizens by moral ones contracted in the camp and field . . . Many thousand blooming damsels, capable and well inclined to serve the state as wives and mothers, were compelled to lead lives of barren celibacy by the siege of Louisburg."[61]

In spite of his fame as a writer, Hawthorne's analysis is lacking in this instance. Yes, Louisbourg cost lives, but only 4,500 men went with Pepperrell and the majority returned safe and sound. Many thousands of other young men never left their homes at all. Many others returned as military veterans, possessing talents that would be used or shared to eventually win independence for the United States. Going to Louisbourg eventually became an act of courage and a badge of honor for all who did it.

All things do come to an end. For Pepperrell, the beginning of the end of his time at Louisbourg came in April 1746, when the Baronet received permission to go home. He and his men still had to wait for the Gibraltar regiments to arrive; but they were on the way. Once they

---

[61] Hawthorne.

"To The Uttermost Of My Power"

arrived, he and his men could go home. He had been at Louisbourg long enough.[62]

On May 19, 1745, Warren and Pepperrell said good-bye to a large contingent of troops going home. Warren told Pepperrell's citizen-soldiers they had won the victory here. He told Pepperrell and his men, he hoped "the same spirit that induced you to make the Conquest will prompt you to keep it."[63]

All told, the experience of Louisbourg seemed to conflict Pepperrell. He understood what he and the New England Land Forces had done. He had taken untrained militia to reduce the greatest fortress on a continent. The militia had coalesced and forged a fighting force. Together they had completed the assignment in 49 days. It truly astonished everyone.

Yet he seemed surprised and hurt by Shirley's jealousy and by some of the ways the Governor treated him. I don't think he ever understood it. After all, it took him nearly a decade to even acknowledge it.

Shirley's problem was he could not be in two places at once. He truly wanted the command himself, but he knew only he could handle the work in Boston. He

---

[62] Most New Englanders were extremely proud of the work they did at Louisbourg. Those who accompanied Pepperrell north to conquest were honored for the rest of their days, and veterans were proud of their service. Boston commemorated the victory of the Provincial forces by naming part of its prestigious Beacon Hill residential district "Louisbourg Square." The name is still in use.
[63] Parkman, p. 668.

"To The Uttermost Of My Power"

certainly didn't want Sir William to fail; but he didn't want him to make it look so easy. When much of the credit rightly went to Pepperrell, it woke up the jealousy in Shirley.

Pepperrell's sole fault was being rewarded for what he had done, and Shirley had no control over those awards. No matter what anyone, anywhere said, Pepperrell's achievement was monumental. Louisbourg and the Plains of Abraham in 1759 were the two most significant military victories in the history of pre-revolutionary British North America.

The next victory in the New World of comparable magnitude would come 32 years later at a small New York village called Saratoga.

"To The Uttermost Of My Power"

Chapter XIV

A Return Triumphant

ONCE HE RECEIVED PERMISSION, PEPPERRELL WASTED LITTLE TIME GETTING READY TO HEAD BACK TO NEW ENGLAND.

Admiral Warren was ready to go as well. He had resigned the governorship of Cape Breton Island in anticipation of a new Navy assignment and, he too, was eager to leave Louisbourg behind him.

Both men loaded their trunks and other personal items on board the *Chester*, the flagship of Commodore Charles Knowles, who was replacing Admiral Warren as both governor and naval commander at Louisbourg. The *Chester* would bring them to Boston as quickly as possible. Finally, on July 4, 1746, the ship set sail for Massachusetts.

Commodore Knowles, meanwhile, had quickly decided he hated the remoteness of the place. He hated the assignment in general and pestered London continually to be given a command at sea. Shortly before Pepperrell and Warren left, on July 1, 1746, he wrote a scathing indictment of the New England troops he had under his command to the Duke of Newcastle.

First of all, he told Newcastle he despised the New Englander's lack of work ethic -- he believed that every

"To The Uttermost Of My Power"

one of them made their living from selling rum. That included their general as well. Knowles also found the New Englanders dirty, unkempt, profane, lazy, undependable, traitorous, and disgusting. He even said he much preferred the industriousness of the French settlers compared to the laziness of the New Englanders. This would not be his last conflict with New England.

Pepperrell and Warren spent most of the time at sea together, and this only helped to solidify their friendship. No doubt when the *Chester* passed the Piscataqua estuary, Sir William was tempted to order Captain Spry to turn the ship into Portsmouth harbor so he could get home that much sooner. But the *Chester* sailed right past the mouth of the river and skirted the Isles of Shoals where Sir William's father had started his business. On June 1, the *Chester* reached Boston and began to make its way through the islands dotting the city's harbor.

If Pepperrell had any questions about what kind of a reception he would be given, they were answered quickly. As the ship neared the town, cannon began to boom from Castle William in tribute to the two men. Batteries on other islands and the mainland answered those guns until the clear harbor sky was clouded by gunpowder smoke.

Boats flying colorful flags and carrying a variety of colony dignitaries came out to meet the *Chester*, and a large welcoming crowd was waiting on the docks to salute Pepperrell and Warren as they left the ship.

As the British warship tied up at Long Wharf, Pepperrell saw a large group of people waiting for them. Led by Governor Shirley, the group included the entire General

"To The Uttermost Of My Power"

Court and the Governor's Council. The crowd roared in tribute to the men and their achievements as Pepperrell and Warren walked down the gangplank.

Shirley greeted each man warmly with a sincere handshake and smiled broadly as the crowd cheered. The streets leading to Province House (today's Old State House Historic Site) were lined on both sides with members of the Governor's Guard and the King's Regiment, both units of the Boston militia.

Then the three heroes -- Pepperrell, Warren and Shirley -- walked through the throng and made their way up King's Street. All along the route, people filled balconies, windows and rooftops to cheer the conquerors of Louisbourg.

Once they reached Province House, they went directly to Pepperrell's Council Chamber, where he was quickly re-elected to the presidency of the body. The Baronet gladly took his old seat at the table.

Later that day, the General Court invited the two men to their chamber for a small ceremony. Thomas Cushing, the Speaker of the House, then made a presentation.

"The House of Representatives of this Province," Cushing said, "have a high sense of the services you have done for his Majesty's subjects in general and the people of New England in particular; and it is with the greatest pleasure that we embrace this happy opportunity for your acknowledgment of it. In their name and on their behalf, I congratulate you and take this opportunity for you to acknowledge our gratitude."

"To The Uttermost Of My Power"

Admiral Warren, replete in his blue and white naval uniform, rose from his seat near the council table to respond. "Mr. Speaker, I am obliged to this honorable House for the great respect they have shown me," he said. "They may depend on my zeal and service while I live for the colonies in general and this one in particular."

Then Lieutenant General Pepperrell rose said a few words. "Mr. Speaker I am heartily obliged to the honorable House for the respect they have shown me and I shall always be ready to risk my life and my fortune for the good of my dear native country."[64]

The chamber then broke into a loud round of applause. After a reception where the members of the legislature had the opportunity to speak to the General and the Admiral, the pair went to dine with Shirley.

No one knows what the three talked about at dinner, but there can be little doubt they reviewed the siege of Louisbourg in the most positive terms. In many ways, a microcosm of the British Empire sat at the table that evening. There was Shirley, the overlord of Louisbourg as well as Massachusetts, the organizer of victory and the representative of the Crown. Then there was Admiral Warren, representing the professional soldiers and sailors who founded the Empire and who defended it with their lives. Finally, there was Pepperrell, the man of America who defended his home, built his business, practiced home-rule and who helped lay the seeds for the United States of America. This was the trio who had turned a mad scheme into an incredible victory.

---

[64] Parsons, p. 141.

"To The Uttermost Of My Power"

Warren stayed in Boston for several days and enjoyed a number of celebratory banquets and receptions. He then bade a sad farewell to Pepperrell and boarded a warship for his trip back to England, where his next assignment would be with the Royal Navy's Channel Fleet.

After Warren left, Sir William spent several days cleaning up work from the fifteen months he missed while commanding at Louisbourg. He spent pleasant nights in the familiar comfort of his house on Boston's Summer Street.

Finally, on July 4, 1746, Sir William was ready to go home to Kittery Point. He set out from Boston right after breakfast accompanied by several of his officers and gentlemen who were also going in the same direction. When his party got to the border of the town of Lynn, crowds of citizens and the mounted militia met him in joyous celebration. After a brief stop, the group was escorted to the nearby city of Salem.

In a city not so long ago dominated by witches, he was greeted by a cannon salute and church bells rang throughout the city in his honor. The crowd of well-wishers, which filled the town green, then escorted Sir William to the town hall where a great banquet and entertainment awaited to honor the victorious Baronet.

After dinner toasts were made to honor, among others, King George II, Governor Shirley, Sir William, Admiral Warren, Major General Wolcott, Brigadier General Waldo and others. When each name was called, a cannon was fired in tribute. Mounted militia then escorted Pepperrell to the Beverly ferry. On reaching the opposite shore, a cavalcade of militia and citizens escorted the Baronet through Ipswich and on to Newbury, where his arrival

"To The Uttermost Of My Power"

was announced by brilliant fireworks and cannon salutes at 11 PM. He then spent the night at the home of Major John Greenleaf.

Next morning, July 5, Sir William arose at the Greenleaf house and began the last day of his journey home. He forded the Merrimac River and shortly thereafter, crossed the imaginary line that separated Massachusetts and its northern neighbor and entered the Province of New Hampshire and continued north.

In Hampton, Pepperrell was greeted by two companies of mounted militia; the High Sheriff of Rockingham County; and the entire provincial council. They rode on with him to Portsmouth, where the procession went to the Little Harbour mansion of his sometime friend, sometime nemesis and one-time tent merchant, Governor Benning Wentworth. Like old friends, Pepperrell and Wentworth had a long, quiet and very uneventful dinner.

The sun had been down for sometime when Pepperrell boarded Wentworth's barge for the trip across the river.

William Pepperrell, who went to Louisbourg with 100 ships and 4,500 soldiers, came home alone.

His favorite reception no doubt took place when Governor Wentworth's barge tied up at the dock at Pepperrell Cove. There is no record of who met him there, but it was probably his wife Mary, now Lady Pepperrell; his son Andrew; his daughter Betsy and son-in-law Nathaniel Sparhawk; their children and the household servants and slaves. It must have been a joyous, tearful, heart-felt reunion.

The conqueror of Louisbourg was home.

"To The Uttermost Of My Power"

Chapter XV

"Hold Fire!"

NOT LONG AFTER PEPPERRELL RETURNED HOME, RUMORS BEGAN TO CIRCULATE IN NEW ENGLAND ABOUT A LARGE FRENCH BATTLE FLEET EMBARKING A NEWLY RAISED ARMY AT BREST, FRANCE.

The rumors said the fleet would include 40 newly built men-of-war, including heavily gunned ships-of-the-line. The goal of this armada was simple -- retake Louisbourg.

King Louis XV was furious about the loss of the fortress and he was insisting that it be recovered by the force of French arms. The King even remembered Boston.

New rumors indicated that if the French were victorious at Louisbourg, they might bring to fruition a long-feared nightmare, sail down the coast, and attack an open and vulnerable Boston. King Louis wanted his fleet to leave the city a burning, smoking ghost town. He entrusted the expedition to the 37-year-old Duc d'Anville.

Louisbourg was no longer Pepperrell's direct concern even though his regiment, the 51st Foot, was stationed there. But the York County militia was his responsibility, and he made sure troops were prepared and coastal defenses strengthened.

Militia from all over New England were mobilized and many troops marched on Boston to help provide defense for that city. All told, some six thousand militiamen arrived to help with the crisis.

"To The Uttermost Of My Power"

In a September 1746 letter to fellow councilor and long-time friend Samuel Waldo, Pepperrell outlined another worry he had. "I am concerned about the province of Maine; am afraid it will be lost if the war holds out long; without there is some care taken of it. I should think it would now be good time to build a fort at Penobscot; pray think of it and put it forward if you are of that opinion."[65]

The fort at Penobscot, at the mouth of the river with the same name, was an idea that Pepperrell had long advocated as a way to show strength in eastern Maine and as a way to defend local settlements. The proposal for the fort was defeated every year until 1759, the year of Pepperrell's death.

MEANWHILE, THE NAVAL THREAT OF 1746 CAME TO NAUGHT.

It was real enough; the fleet left France with 68 ships -- including several with more than 90 guns. The ships carried thousands of soldiers, all trained to make amphibious landings that would be required at Louisbourg. The unfortunate fleet ran into an ocean storm, which tore the French armada to pieces. Then, in a stroke of amazing bad luck, the battered survivors ran into a second, equally powerful storm in the mouth of the St. Lawrence River. The fleet was almost totally destroyed.

When the surviving captains were summoned to the flagship for a conference, they asked the Duke what they should do now. The young admiral had no answers for them. In fact, after the conference, he went below decks to his cabin and committed suicide.

---

[65] Parsons, Pepperrell to Waldo, September 4, 1746, p. 153.

"To The Uttermost Of My Power"

At the same time as this naval threat, the colonial authorities were looking to counter danger from the west. Governor Shirley was trying to raise an Army to attack Fort St. Frederic at Crown Point on Lake Champlain and then perhaps move on Quebec itself. Pepperrell helped to pass the plan through the General Court, even though he was left out of the command structure. But the Duke of Newcastle later rejected the project as too costly.

By now Shirley's jealousy of Pepperrell began to grow more obvious. In the convoluted prose of the day, Shirley wrote to the Duke of Newcastle that though he was superior in rank to Pepperrell politically, he felt inferior socially because he was not a baronet. He hoped the situation would be resolved. It never was to Shirley's satisfaction -- he never became a baronet.

Once he arrived back in New England, Sir William was a very busy man. In addition to his legislative duties in Boston, he rejoined the Court of Common Pleas as a judge again; he picked up his duties as head of the Maine militia; he was still involved in other things with Kittery's local government. He also struck up an ongoing relationship with the new minister of his church at Kittery Point, Rev. Benjamin Stevens, now co-pastor with Rev. Newmarch. As if this was not enough to do, others found more work for him.

Since he had been a frequent correspondent with the Admiralty during the Louisburg campaign, the London Sea Lords were aware of Pepperrell's talents and experience. Using Admiral Warren as an intermediary, they wrote to him in late 1746 to ask that he gather materials for and supervise the construction of a new 44-gun Navy frigate to be built in the Piscataqua area. It

"TO THE UTTERMOST OF MY POWER"

was one of four new ships to be built for the Royal Navy in the colonies.

In March of 1747, Pepperrell contacted Benning Wentworth in Portsmouth on the matter, and the Governor had his suppliers gather the wood, masts, rope, sails, cordage and tons of other items they would need to construct the warship.

Pepperrell supervised the building of the ship in the Piscataqua basin at the Portsmouth shipyard of Nathaniel Meserve, who also had gone to Louisbourg with a New Hampshire regiment and who had solved the problem of getting the guns across the marshes.

Once a week, the Baronet crossed the Piscataqua to inspect the work carefully. When the hull was complete and with only one mast in place, the ship was loaded with spars, yards and everything needed for a proper fitting out. On May 4, 1748, the ship was completed and ready to be sent to England. She was then escorted to England for the rest of the fitting out. The resulting vessel -- *America* -- had a brief career in the Royal Navy. Well-built, she was known as a good sailing ship, but due to some modifications on her design made by Commodore Charles Knowles, wood was overexposed to the elements and rot set in. Not long after her commissioning, *America* was condemned and taken out of service.

In an interesting side note, *America* played host to a unique meeting while it was being built. During the colonial era, the Portsmouth/Kittery region was a center of Freemasonry. Eventually four distinct Masonic lodges -- three in Portsmouth and a fourth in Kittery -- were created to handle local membership. Shipbuilder Nathaniel Meserve belonged to the oldest one -- St.

"To The Uttermost Of My Power"

John's Lodge in Portsmouth -- and he arranged to hold a lodge meeting on board the ship to show it off to members and to use it to recruit new members. It appears it was a well-attended meeting. Although Masonry was popular in the colonies, there is no indication Pepperrell was ever a member.

In spite of the fate of this one vessel, American shipyards continued to produce superior fighting ships, particularly frigates, as evidenced by the performance of the U.S.S. *Constitution* during the War of 1812.

PEPPERRELL NOW RAN INTO PROBLEMS WITH HIS REGIMENT, THE 51ST FOOT, which was serving at Louisbourg along with Shirley's 50th Foot, as well as the two regiments of redcoats from Gibraltar. For some reason, Army officials in London had appointed a William Ryan as the lieutenant colonel of Pepperrell's regiment without consulting the Baronet. The lieutenant colonel in a regiment is especially important because he is the executive officer and normally runs the formation when the colonel is absent, which, in those days, was almost all the time.

Pepperrell understood it was the Army's right to name the second-in-command, but he was upset he had not been consulted because he had practically offered the post to his old friend Lt. Col. John Bradstreet. Now Bradstreet would be forced to perhaps take a less prestigious posting with a lesser regiment.

Bradstreet, a long-time friend of Pepperrell's, eventually was named lieutenant governor of Nova Scotia and governor of Newfoundland.

Then in December, while the Baronet was at home in Kittery, he received a letter from Commodore Knowles,

"To The Uttermost Of My Power"

the governor of Louisbourg. Knowles had smelled a rat and he had discovered irregularities in the officers' commissions for the 51st Foot presented to him by Lt. Colonel Ryan. It was obvious someone had tampered with the documents; names had been substituted and changed; dates had been rewritten to impact seniority. All the evidence pointed to Ryan as the sole suspect in the incident.

It had been Pepperrell's job, as colonel and sponsor of the regiment to distribute the commissions to officers of his choice. In most cases, the commissions were literally sold to people. This was standard procedure for most regiments and it was the way that colonels, like Pepperrell and Shirley, could obtain the financial rewards promised by having their own regiments.

Pepperrell had done that, although some of the commissions he returned to the Army headquarters in London were blank. Pepperrell planned to take care of them at a later date. Ryan had apparently sold some of the blank commissions himself and pocketed the money. Pepperrell wrote back to Knowles that he had never even heard of some of the men who now claimed they were officers of his regiment.

Further questioning of some of the officers provided enough evidence for Knowles and the Army to take action. Lt. Colonel Ryan was charged with tampering and the illegal selling of Army commissions. He faced a court martial at Louisbourg where he was found guilty and then was dishonorably discharged from the Army.

Pepperrell took a great deal of pride in being the colonel of his own regiment in the British Army and this action by Ryan deeply embarrassed the Kittery merchant. He later successfully sued Ryan for defamation of character.

"To The Uttermost Of My Power"

But the history of the 51st Foot was not distinguished and it would be further sullied in the French and Indian War. It would not be the fault of Sir William.

IN EARLY 1747, THE FRENCH SENT ANOTHER LARGE FLEET OF 38 SHIPS ACROSS THE ATLANTIC TO ATTEMPT TO RETAKE LOUISBOURG. This time, the English didn't depend on the weather to disrupt the attack plans. The Admiralty dispatched Admirals Warren and George Anson with a fleet of ships to rebuff that threat. The two fleets met on May 3 and Warren and Anson soundly defeated the French in a running sea battle off Cape Finisterre. For his service in the sea fight, Warren was raised to a baronetcy, which delighted his old friend in Kittery.

Pepperrell wrote to Warren on September 16, 1747, from Louisbourg; "Hearing of your good success against the French fleet, and the honor conferred on you as baronet, has given me such pleasure as I cannot find words to express."[66]

Pepperrell also kept a captaincy in the 51st Foot open for a relative of Admiral Warren's from the colony of New York. Warren Johnson was the son of Sir William Johnson, chief Indian agent for British North America and Admiral Warren's nephew.

DURING THE TURMOIL OVER HIS REGIMENT, PEPPERRELL WENT TO LOUISBOURG TO ATTEND LT. COLONEL RYAN'S COURT martial. When it was over, he returned to Boston from the north on the flagship of the now -- Admiral Charles Knowles, who was leaving his post as governor to assume a naval command.

---

[66] Parsons, Pepperrell to Warren, September 10, 1747, p. 166.

"To The Uttermost Of My Power"

On September 24, sailing south to Boston, the fleet ran into yet another tremendous storm damaging several ships. The *Warwick* lost all three of her masts; the *Canterbury* had to jettison 16 guns for safety's sake; the *Achilles* had to cut away her main mast; and the *Essex* lost three guns. The fleet made it to Boston, and then anchored at Nantasket Roads to refit and repair. It would take some time to get the work done.

While in the provincial capital, 16 British sailors deserted their ships, a situation that infuriated Admiral Knowles, whose temper was famous throughout the Royal Navy and who had already formed negative opinions about New Englanders.

Knowles and his fleet anchored off Nantasket Roads as his damaged ships were slowly repaired by Boston shipwrights. He was waiting for a convoy of merchant ships to arrive and then he was to escort them to England. But now Knowles needed more men to make up for those deserters. To get men, he acted as he would have in England -- he sent press gangs into the nearest population center to get men. He sent the *Lark* into Boston. She tied up at Long Wharf and then the press gangs started their work on November 17, 1747.

Press gangs were armed parties of sailors who, in England, had the legal right to grab any healthy looking civilians they could find and drag them away to unspecified terms in the Navy. On that day in November 1747, they pressed a number of local Boston dockyard workers and brought them out to the fleet at Nantasket Roads in various stages of unconsciousness.

The news of the impressments spread rapidly throughout the city, and a mob of nearly 300 disgruntled sailors, dockworkers and outraged citizens began to form on the

"To The Uttermost Of My Power"

streets to protest Knowles' action. The mob found several officers from the *Lark*, wandering around Boston and took them into their "protective" custody.

The crowd marched on Province House on King (now State) Street and threw rocks and other objects through the windows. When that accomplished nothing, the mob then stormed to the courthouse, where Pepperrell and the council were meeting. Both Shirley and Pepperrell spoke to the crowd, but they failed to calm them down or get them to disperse.

Later in the day, Pepperrell, the other council members and some militia escorted Shirley to his home in Roxbury, but the mob followed close on their heels. In a report to the Admiralty on the incident, Shirley wrote that his supporters were about to fire on the mob as they tried to burn a barge they had stolen from the harbor on the grounds of the mansion.

Sir William saw what was about to happen and he knew he had to try and stop this group from firing into the mob. He ran forward and yelled out in a strong voice, obviously used to command, to "hold fire!" Hearing his voice so full of authority, the riflemen held their fire, preventing a volley of musket balls from ripping into the crowd. The quick reaction by the Baronet probably prevented a massacre in the streets of Boston. Shirley fled to Castle William on the harbor islands and the mob burned the barge on Boston Common.

When Knowles heard of the situation, he again lost his temper and threatened to bring his fleet into the harbor and open fire. That only made the crowd more indignant and determined to have the pressed men released. On the advice of Pepperrell, the Admiral thought better of this plan and backed down.

"To The Uttermost Of My Power"

Known as the Knowles Riot, this disturbance held the town of Boston hostage for three long days. Finally, Bostonians held a special town meeting to tackle the problem. Determined to protect their rights as Englishmen, the assembly condemned Knowles' action and also censured, at Pepperrell's request, the actions of the mob. The citizens and the Royal Navy came to an accommodation, thanks to this effort led by Pepperrell and others.

The pressed men were freed, the angry and frustrated Admiral Knowles got his officers back, and then he sailed away from the "damned" port of Boston. The town's militia reappeared, and Shirley came back from Castle William. Much of this was thanks to Sir William, who might just have prevented an early Boston Massacre.

There was one other person in Boston who took careful mental notes on the Knowles Riot and filed them away in the recesses of his brain for future use. His name was Samuel Adams and he would always remember how useful a mob could be.

In yet another testament to Pepperrell's ability to forgive and forget, he engaged in a lengthy and extremely friendly correspondence with Admiral Knowles shortly after the riot in Boston. Although Sir William had opposed and helped to counter the fiery Knowles in the impressment crisis, it appears he held no grudges or even negative opinions about his adversary in this matter.

As time went by, William Pepperrell could not seem to get away from some of the unfair repercussions from Louisbourg. In 1748, he heard from his agent in London, Christopher Kilby, that a complaint about his

"To The Uttermost Of My Power"

management at the French fortress had been filed with Secretary of State for War. No specific charges were indicated, but Kilby wrote that the claim noted alleged favored treatment of troops from one province over the others; the appointment of incompetent officers; the withholding of pay for no good reason, and other perceived violations of military protocol. Both Pepperrell and Shirley were named in this matter, which could mean trouble if the secretary took it seriously.

Kilby continued to monitor the situation in London and eventually reported back that the government only considered it a payroll dispute and it would have no impact on Baronet Pepperrell or Governor Shirley.

TAKEN IN TOTAL, THERE SEEMED TO BE VERY FEW THINGS PEPPERRELL COULDN'T -- AND DIDN'T DO -- DURING THESE busy years after Louisbourg. His resume at that time included:

- Head of the colony Governor's Council;
- Chief Judge of York County Court;
- Colonel of York County militia;
- Colonel of 51st Regiment of Foot;
- Lt. General of Massachusetts;
- Chief Indian negotiator;
- Chief recruiter from Maine;
- Head of Pepperrell trading business;
- Manager of family land purchases;
- Manager of sawmill operations at several locations;
- Supervised frigate construction;
- Trustee of Congregational Church;
- Involved in local fisheries;
- Voluminous letter-writer.

"To The Uttermost Of My Power"

He was successful at all of them.

SEVERAL TIMES DURING THE POST-LOUISBOURG YEARS, PEPPERRELL EXPRESSED INTEREST IN OBTAINING A ROYAL GOVERNORSHIP AS A fitting capstone to his career of service to the Crown. It was no secret he wanted the governorship of Cape Breton Island that went to Commodore Warren.

One gubernatorial opportunity came up in 1749 right across the river in Portsmouth. After years of putting up with the corruption and hi-jinx of Benning Wentworth, many members of the New Hampshire legislature were fed up and wanted Wentworth replaced. They petitioned the King for Wentworth's removal, and asked Sir William to use any influence he might have now in London since Louisbourg to secure his appointment as governor to replace the corrupt Wentworth.

The Baronet was about to leave on his first trip to England (see Chapter I), but he remained strictly non-committal to the anti-Wentworth forces. Wentworth, however, thought Pepperrell was going to London to lobby King George, to take over the New Hampshire governorship, but this was not the case at all.

Further south in Boston, Governor Shirley grew more and more unpopular towards the end of the decade. A faction in the General Court looked to Pepperrell as an acceptable alternative to the feisty governor -- if the Kittery man would push for the job. But Pepperrell did not wish to seem ungrateful to his patron, and he again remained noncommittal and quiet about the matter. As a result, his elevation to the top job in Massachusetts never took place.

"To The Uttermost Of My Power"

Apparently those who fed the Piscataqua area rumor mills felt the Baronet would discuss these matters in private with the King once he got to England. However, from what is known about Pepperrell's audience with King George II, those talks never took place. Neither did a conversation about a third governorship. That scenario called for Maine to be detached from Massachusetts again to become its own colony and have as its governor -- Sir William Pepperrell.

Pepperrell never became a governor, although he held the Massachusetts post on an acting basis for four months after Shirley was recalled. His son-in-law, Nathaniel Sparhawk, wrote he needed to pursue the goal with more drive and desire. And he was right -- but for the wrong reasons. Sir William didn't have to pursue honors because, for the most part, they pursued him.

His reluctance to strive for the Massachusetts or New Hampshire governorships revealed a lot about Pepperrell's character. He would not betray his patron Shirley, who had given him Louisbourg, and he would not oppose Wentworth, who he seemed to like more and more as time went on. Loyalty and friendship meant a lot to a man who already had plenty of honor.

In 1748, Pepperrell made a major decision about his business. He notified his clients he would not be re-entering the business world and recommended they deal with his son Andrew as the head of The Messrs. William Pepperrell. Much like his father, Sir William planned to devote most of his time to public service.

Also late that year, he caught rheumatic fever and was ill for several weeks. He believed his extended stay at Louisbourg had weakened his overall health and made

"To The Uttermost Of My Power"

him more susceptible to sickness. He never really was able to shake it and this illness would be considered the cause of his death eleven years later.

AS THE YEAR 1748 DREW TO A CLOSE, THE WARRING NATIONS IN EUROPE were finishing up the negotiations which produced the Treaty of Aix-La-Chappelle ending the War of The Austrian Succession and its North American version, King George's War. The treaty did not address many of the conflicts with the principals, and it left enough sparks behind that another war was sure to ignite in a few years. Provincials, however, were incensed when they heard about Louisbourg. Louisbourg, the Gibraltar of the West, was returned lock, stock and barrel to France. It was more like a trade: Louisbourg was given back to France; Madras, India, was given back to Great Britain.

A story current at the time, told about the French asking for the return of Louisbourg at the conference. When asked by the negotiators, King George II said he had no control over it because the people of Boston had taken it and it was theirs. He later changed his mind when he felt more things were at stake than the feelings of the Provincials. There is little doubt the King underestimated the feelings of those New Englanders, the same mistake his grandson, King George III, would make some two decades later.

The Provincials in Boston and throughout New England were livid when Louisbourg became French again. The Massachusetts General Court blasted the treaty, which basically restored the status quo before the war. There is little doubt this blatant disregard of what the Provincials did helped to start the change in attitudes

"To The Uttermost Of My Power"

toward the Mother Country and monarch that came to a head in 1776.

Strangely, there was little reaction to be found from Sir William, though he must not have been pleased. All that effort, all those deaths now seemed like nothing. The end of the war also meant the disbandment of the Shirley and Pepperrell regiments, which disappointed both men.

In August of 1749, Pepperrell did mention Louisbourg in a letter to Peter Kenwood, his primary merchant in London. "As we understand," Pepperrell wrote in his elegant hand, "Louisbourg is to be delivered to its former owners," noting also that English settlers were moving into what would become Halifax in Nova Scotia. He also admitted that he had expended a large portion of his fortune on a large portion of his wealth on underwriting the Louisbourg venture and he was hoping to obtain reimbursement for himself and others on his coming trip to London. He told Kenwood he regretted that the 51st Foot was being disbanded, and he reiterated a desire to leave the business world behind and "become a farmer." But of Louisbourg, he said very little.[67]

IN THE MEANTIME, THERE WAS GOOD NEWS ON THE FINANCIAL FRONT FROM LONDON. Parliament, through the good offices of Peter Warren, now a member, was getting closer to approving the funds to FINALLY reimburse the colonies for the Louisbourg expedition. So far, the colonies had been waiting for more than five years to get the reimbursement. One of the reasons Pepperrell was going to England was to meet with Warren and check over and approve the appropriate accounts and ledgers.

---

[67] Parsons, Pepperrell to Kenwood, August 13, 1749, p. 207.

"To The Uttermost Of My Power"

He would have two pleasant reunions with the Admiral that he remembered to his dying day.

Thanks to the work done by the old comrades, Parliament finally voted to reimburse the colonies for the Louisbourg expedition -- more than 600,000 gold coins distributed proportionately among the colonies and the men. One would assume the Baronet was reimbursed for the 10,000 pounds he spent out of his own pocket.

But it must not have been the full amount because in 1757, Pepperrell filed a final petition with the General Court seeking reimbursement. The body approved the petition and Pepperrell received 188 pounds in back salary and 1,000 pounds in expenses. Always the businessman, the Baronet never forgot what was his due.

"To The Uttermost Of My Power"

Chapter XVI

A Great Bereavement

WHEN WILLIAM PEPPERRELL RETURNED FROM ENGLAND IN 1750, HE INTENDED TO REAFFIRM HIS DECISION ANNOUNCED IN 1748 TO LET HIS SON CONTINUE TO RUN THE TRADING AND SHIPPING PORTION OF THE BUSINESS.

The Baronet would keep control over the land purchasing and spend more of his time in public service in Boston and Kittery.

But, in fact, he began to pay a bit more attention to the family business. Not that it was in trouble, but both he and Lady Mary were beginning to be a little concerned about Andrew.

The Pepperrell's only surviving son, Andrew, had become a full partner in the family business, finally taking full control when his father left for Louisbourg in 1745. Five years later, Andrew was in total control of the shipping and general trading business, while Sir William controlled the family's land operations. But the Baronet thought things could be better in the Pepperrell enterprises.

Andrew Pepperrell was born into wealth and privilege as the first son of Mary and William Pepperrell. Both parents acknowledged the value inherent in education, and Andrew received most of his in Boston rather than at the smaller Kittery schools as his father had attended. Andrew's education was the best money could buy in colonial America.

"To The Uttermost Of My Power"

By the time he was 15, Andrew was enrolled at Harvard College in Cambridge, Massachusetts. When he graduated in 1743, he ranked second in his class. It should be noted, however, that in those days, class rankings were based on social status, not academic achievement. The class rank does show the esteem with which the Pepperrells were held in the Boston social establishment.

Andrew was enthusiastic and energetic when he took over control of the Pepperrell trading company. He was methodical in his operations and gave the impression of being a thorough, detail-oriented manager.

He hired captains and bought and sold ships. He selected trade routes, and decided on merchandise to sell. Like his father and grandfather, Andrew joined in Kittery town activities, and he served on several town boards and committees.

Andrew, of course, couldn't learn everything about such a complicated business as that run by his father. He was helped by his brother-in-law, Nathaniel Sparhawk, who worked closely with Andrew while his father prepared for Louisbourg. Sparhawk was able to teach the budding merchant a great deal about the colonial business world, while running his own firm of Sparhawk & Colman.

When he returned from Europe, however, Sir William noticed Andrew would often ignore advice or do just the opposite of what he suggested. Andrew also ignored his parents and decided to build a separate house for himself and his prospective bride-to-be not far from the Pepperrell Mansion. Sir William and his wife sensed a wall growing between them and their son.

"To The Uttermost Of My Power"

Then there were the huge question marks surrounding Andrew's impending marriage to Hannah Waldo, daughter of General Samuel Waldo, one of Sir William's best friends.

Shortly after leaving Harvard, Andrew announced his engagement to Miss Waldo. Both families were delighted by the betrothal between the sole heir to one of the colony's largest fortunes and a young woman who was described as "highly educated, accomplished and beautiful."

This marriage would legally entwine two of the leading merchant families in Massachusetts, not to mention reuniting two old war comrades and two old friends. It seemed like a perfect match.

But then month after month passed and no wedding date was forthcoming. Twice dates were fixed and twice Andrew postponed them. Then more months passed. Waldo and Pepperrell exchanged letters, and both were perplexed with what was wrong with Andrew. Pepperrell wrote in one letter to Waldo that he couldn't imagine his son living without Hannah.

But obviously Andrew could.

In March, 1750, Nathaniel Sparhawk wrote: "The love affair between Andrew Pepperrell and Miss Waldo, now of four years duration, is still pending much to the annoyance of both families as well as trying of the patience of the young lady."[68]

Stephen Minot, a fellow merchant in Boston, also wrote to Andrew hoping for a happy conclusion to the matter.

---

[68] Parsons, p. 217.

"TO THE UTTERMOST OF MY POWER"

"I hope my friend, it will not be long before we see you in town to disappoint the enemies as well as to complete the approaching pleasure which you have in view of enjoying the society of so charming and desirable a lady as Miss Hannah."[69]

By now four years had gone by since the engagement was announced. Andrew and Hannah set a third date. Once again, he tried to postpone the wedding, but Hannah would allow no more delay.

According to those who were there, the two families gathered in Boston for the wedding. Everyone was in their place and anxiously awaiting the ceremonies. Then the bride, Hannah Waldo, walked in and said she would never marry Andrew Pepperrell. Then she walked out. Within weeks, Hannah was married to Thomas Flucker, the secretary of the province.

Neither Andrew nor Hannah would ever publicly mention this social disaster. General Waldo was furious, not at the principals but mostly about the overall embarrassment of it. The Baronet and Lady Pepperrell were disappointed and "chagrined" by the way things developed, but the Waldo/Pepperrell friendship continued.

Andrew Pepperrell blamed his reluctance to marry on a chronic fever he had contracted some time ago, and because of serious business setbacks he had suffered when several of his ships were lost at sea.

He also argued that his intentions toward Hannah were honorable, and he pointed out the new house he had

---

[69] Parsons, Stephen Minot to Andrew Pepperrell, June 3, 1750 p. 219.

"To The Uttermost Of My Power"

built near his parent's home as proof of that. The cost of the new house he built for Hannah also demonstrated his intentions. Andrew spent 10,000 pounds of his own money, plus 8,000 pounds he borrowed from his father to build the home.

Whatever the reason, Andrew had turned a pleasant arrangement in matrimony into a complete social disaster.

IN THE END, BOTH HANNAH AND ANDREW WERE STAR-CROSSED, TRAGIC FIGURES.

Thomas and Hannah Flucker had a daughter, Lucy, who in 1775 married Henry Knox, the owner of The London Book Store in Boston. Her parents were not pleased because Knox was a Patriot while the Fluckers were confirmed Loyalists. Shortly after the skirmishes at Lexington and Concord, the Fluckers packed up what they could and fled to London.

They never saw Lucy again.

Lucy's husband did very well for himself, however. Escaping from Boston, he joined the besieging Continental Army. Knox helped end the siege of Boston by leading a contingent of soldiers who dragged artillery overland on sleds from Fort Ticonderoga in New York. The Continental Congress named him a major general and George Washington appointed him to be the Continental Army's chief of artillery. The man he succeeded as head of artillery was none other than Richard Gridley, Pepperrell's gunnery chief at Louisbourg.

At the end of the Revolution, Knox succeeded Washington as commander-in-chief of the Continental

"TO THE UTTERMOST OF MY POWER"

Army. He was also the first Secretary of War in Washington's cabinet. After serving his country well, Henry and Lucy Knox later retired to Montpelier[70], their extensive estate near the mouth of the Penobscot River in Thomaston, Maine.

From the Pepperrell perspective, it is hard to believe, but things got worse -- much worse.

On February 20, 1751, Andrew attended a party in Portsmouth. Apparently he had a good time and stayed until the early morning hours before he decided to go home. While crossing the freezing Piscataqua, he caught a chill, which became a fever, probably typhoid.

The Piscataqua is no gentle, pastoral stream. It really is unlike any other river in the region, broad, flat and wide. In its deep channels, water swirls rapidly in eddies and whirlpools, which make it impossible to safely ford or even attempt to swim. According to modern measures, it is the third fastest-flowing navigable river in the world.

The senior Pepperrells were consumed with worry. His parents brought in the best doctors in the region and had ministers pray for his recovery. But it was to no avail. He lingered for ten days, distraught and burning with fever, and then on March 1, 1751, Andrew died at the Pepperrell mansion.

He was just 26 years old -- even younger than his uncle Andrew was when he so suddenly died. His obituary appeared in the *Boston Evening Post* and his virtues listed showed just a portion of the Pepperrell's loss.

---

[70] The Montpelier mansion has been reconstructed and today it exists as The General Henry Knox Museum in Thomaston, ME.

"To The Uttermost Of My Power"

PORTSMOUTH, March 14. On the 1st instant died at Kittery, at the seat of the Honourable William Pepperrell, Baronet, his only son, Andrew Pepperrell, esq., in the 26th year of his life, and on the 7th Instant, his remains were interred in a manner suited to the superior condition of the family.

He was a young gentleman happy in his natural temper; cheerful, friendly, and social in his make up; of that unaffected sincerity and openness of heart, which are the marks of thorough honesty; not without the prudence and caution, which proceed from some knowledge of the world.

His treatment of mankind was inoffensive and engaging; respectful to his superiors; obliging to his friends and acquaintances, condescending and easy to those below him; free from that assuming and haughty behavior towards inferiors, which gives reason to suspect want of respect and want of breeding. But what is yet more excellent, it was not in his heart to despise the poor; on the contrary, he felt a tender sympathy for them, and his unrequested charities frequently prevented their cries. Such sharers were they of heaven's bounty to him that he might as properly be said to be their steward and benefactor.

He was allowed by good judges to be happy with the powers of his mind; and had not the inclination led him into an extensive trade in which he was eminent for capacity, industry and integrity, he might have distinguished himself by his acquaintance with the arts and sciences for which a good foundation was laid by his liberal education.

He was early instructed in the principles of religion; nor did he want very near him some eminent examples for the practice of it, which had a good effect on him and appeared in his dutifulness to his parents, his constant attendance on the public worship of God his zeal of the settlement of a gospel minister and his ambition for his honorable support. In short, he promised to be a most useful member of society and a still greater blessing to mankind, but alas, a premature death cut off our hopes and expectations."[71]

---

[71] Parsons, Andrew Pepperrell obituary, p. 264.

"To The Uttermost Of My Power"

ANDREW'S DEATH NEARLY BROKE his parents' hearts. Lady Mary withdrew from outside activities; Sir William neglected his council duties in Boston, and he failed to attend several Indian conferences. He turned court cases down with regularity. He wrote letters and saw people but many of his acquaintances said the Baronet was just a shadow of his former self.

As late as June of 1751, the Baronet was still grief-stricken. He wrote to the General Court seeking to postpone a hearing at which he was scheduled to appear. "The Dispensations of Divine Providence towards me and my family," he wrote, "render it almost impossible for me to attend to my duty in this affair or the more important affairs of this Province until my mind is in some greater measure relieved."[72]

Prior to that, on April 26 and after many delays, he finally sat down and wrote to his friend Admiral Warren. The words must have come hard. Pepperrell wrote about his trip to England, saying "A great mercy that I was preserved abroad and returned in health."

Then he continued: "But that mercies and prosperity are not always to be our experiences, I have been lately taught. For on the first day of March, my dear and only son, after an illness of nervous fever of ten days, a healthy, strong and promising young man was taken from us by death -- a very great bereavement. I hope you and your lady never meet with so great a bereavement, and trial."[73]

The Baronet must have greatly missed his son, whom he considered the future of the family and its business.

---

[72] Parsons, Pepperrell to Council, June 19, 1751, p. 238.
[73] Parsons, Pepperrell to Warren, April 26, 1751, p. 236.

"To The Uttermost Of My Power"

Andrew's death forced Sir William to change his mind about being less involved in he business -- he was once again the man in charge. He never was able to find anyone to replace his son.

No doubt the Baronet must have thought of the good working and personal relationship he had with his father. It must have saddened him tremendously to realize he would never have one such as that with his own son.

After Andrew's passing, Pepperrell's son-in-law, Nathaniel Sparhawk, handled some functions in the business, as did his nephew Charles Chauncey. Pepperrell, however, continued to keep control over the business.

DEATH WAS A CONSTANT COMPANION TO ALL settlers on the frontier, to all people in colonial America, at any age. Disease often ran rampant -- an epidemic could strike at any time; sanitary conditions were often minimal; and, for those on the fringes of civilization, a sudden arrow or tomahawk could take their life in an instant. Oftentimes, in heart-rending sadness, parents would end up burying their entire brood of children before they, too, passed away. And a family's socio-economic position made not a bit of difference when a new disease or fever struck a settlement. Medicine was far from an exact science in those days, and most treatments for any disease still consisted of bleedings to eliminate "humors" in the blood or the applications of medicine packs or plasters to affected parts of the body. Medical cure rates were not good to say the least.

Sir William was no stranger to death. Both of his parents lived to a ripe old age, but he had lost his

"TO THE UTTERMOST OF MY POWER"

brother Andrew at 32. And three of his four children had already passed away.

In May of that same year -- 1751 -- Governor Benning Wentworth of New Hampshire lost his own son, Foster. In fact, all of Wentworth's six children predeceased the Governor and his wife. Pepperrell knew the pain Wentworth was feeling and he took it upon himself to console the old fraud of Portsmouth.

On June 10, he wrote to the master of Little Harbour, the Wentworth estate, expressing his sympathy and outlining his faith in God's judgment:

> I sincerely and sensibly sympathize with your Excellency and your sorrowful lady in the loss of your dear son. What shall we say to those things? God is wise and holy and just and good in all his ways and works. Why should a living man complain for the punishment for his sins? Let us search and try our ways and turn to the Lord. May all see our profiting.
>
> William Pepperrell, bart.
>
> I ask your acceptance of a piece of fine venison out of my own inclosure.[74]

Wentworth apparently accepted and enjoyed the deer meat.

Then by the end of the following year, Pepperrell was dealt another blow when he learned his old comrade in conquest, retired Admiral Peter Warren, had died unexpectedly in Ireland. In a November 1752 letter to Lady Warren, Pepperrell fondly recalled the life of his friend the Admiral.

---

[74] Parsons, Pepperrell to Wentworth, August 10, 1751, p. 243.

"To The Uttermost Of My Power"

"My lady" he wrote, "I do heartily sympathize with you in your sorrow for the death of my honored and dear friend, your late beloved husband, New England's friend. May we pray always and remember each other in our daily addresses to the Throne of Christ, social and solitary."

That same year, in April, Pepperrell surprised some of his friends by vigorously endorsing the forced removal of the French settlers -- the Acadians -- from Nova Scotia. Brutally forced from their land, many of these Acadians moved to Louisiana, where they became known as "Cajuns."

To his friends, this was out of character for the kindly Pepperrell to endorse such "ethnic cleansing" to use a 21st century phrase. Never before had he condemned the French like this; normally he was sympathetic to their plight. Such action may well have been a reaction to Andrew's passing as many thought back in those days.

MUCH LIKE HIS FATHER AND MOTHER WHEN HIS BROTHER ANDREW DIED, the Baronet and Lady Pepperrell now sought comfort in their parish church at Kittery Point. Pepperrell had always been a pious man, but after Andrew's death, he seemed to take religion even more seriously and wanted to make it an even more important part of his life.

Both Pepperrells found things to their liking in the simple, beautiful sanctuary, and they found comfort in their friendship with Rev. Benjamin Stevens,[75] who

---

[75] Rev. Benjamin Stevens was born in 1720, the son of Rev. Joseph Stevens of Charlestown, Mass., who died when Benjamin was only two. The young Stevens received a doctor of divinity degree from Harvard in 1785. He spent his entire preaching career at Kittery.

"TO THE UTTERMOST OF MY POWER"

preached a special sermon about Andrew the Sunday following the funeral.

Pepperrell also took great pride in knowing and hosting a variety of men of the cloth at his home. Rare was the clergyman who, on passing through Kittery, did not call on him at his mansion.

Perhaps those visiting clergymen enjoyed their visits to the Pepperrell mansion because it gave them access to one of the largest and richest private libraries north of Boston. As we have seen, Pepperrell built up a substantial law library early in his judicial career to make up for his lack of a legal education. Finding books to be a fulfilling pleasure, Pepperrell had his captains bring home regular, substantial increases to his library. In addition to the legal beginnings, the Pepperrell library featured books on religion, history, natural philosophy, the sciences, as well as novels and poetry.

Some of the titles on the Pepperrell's shelves included the complete works of Jonathan Swift; Alexander Pope's translation of *The Iliad; The History of New England; The Universal Dictionary of Arts and Sciences; A Compleat History of The Turks*; and *A Short Introduction To The Art of Navigation*. He also had several works by Daniel Defoe, including *Robinson Crusoe;* the entire collection of Shakespeare's plays; Geoffrey of Monmouth's ecclesiastical *History of England*; and Sir Thomas Mallory's *Le Morte d'Arthur*. In addition, there were numerous well-read versions of the *Bible*.

As the Pepperrell library continued to grow, any unwanted or excess books were given to a movable lending library created by the town government for residents of Kittery's two northern parishes and the southern most one in neighboring York.

"To The Uttermost Of My Power"

During this period, Pepperrell also became an author himself. In 1753, a Boston publisher printed and distributed *Conference With The Penobscot Tribe,* a collection of reports he had made on dealing with the tribe in Maine.

ONE THING WAS CERTAIN ABOUT THE BARONET DURING THIS PERIOD OF TIME -- he was a very wealthy man. Some accounts indicate he had the largest personal fortune in the 13 colonies, and much of that was due to his own effectiveness as a businessman. His fortune was said to be between 200,000 and 300,000 English pounds -- at the time an enormous sum -- a good portion of which was left in a variety of London bank accounts.

One account of Pepperrell noted that his lifestyle was baronial to say the least. "He entertained hospitably at his home in Kittery, which was elegantly furnished. He had a retinue of servants, kept a four-in-six, and had a barge on the river that was manned by a black crew in showy uniforms. He dressed in the manner of the period, in a suit of scarlet cloth trimmed in gold lace and he wore a large powered wig. He was always generous and particularly so with his donations to the Congregational church at Kittery." [76]

In 1753, the Baronet received a special honor from some of his fellow residents of Massachusetts. A group of settlers along the New Hampshire border were creating a new community and it needed a name. A local parson decided it should be named for Sir William and he convinced his fellow citizens to approve the name.

---

[76] Wilson, Fiske, eds. Appleton's Cyclopedia of American Biography, p. 722.

"To The Uttermost Of My Power"

Hence, Pepperell, Massachusetts was born. Yes, it is spelled with only one "r."

SHORTLY AFTER HE BECAME A PARTNER WITH HIS FATHER FOLLOWING BROTHER ANDREW'S DEATH, William purchased 5,500 acres of land on the east side of the Saco River in Maine. He then subdivided the property, keeping the majority for himself, yet selling several subdivisions to help pay for the purchase. Then the Pepperrell company built a sawmill on the Saco and began to harvest much of the wood on the property for lumber to be used in trade. Pepperrell had hoped to extensively develop most of the land once it was cleared of timber, creating a new settlement that he would call Pepperrellborough.

As a result of Louisbourg, his son's death and the re-ignition of the French and Indian War, Sir William had little or no time to play developer for all of this land. However, he had donated several plots to the town of Biddeford that was growing on the west side of the river. Three years after Sir William died, in 1762, the town of Biddeford renamed all of its property on the east side of the Saco "Pepperrellborough."

During the American Revolution, all land remaining in the hands of the Sir William Pepperrell's Loyalist heirs in the Saco River area was confiscated by the Massachusetts state government in 1777. And in 1805, the name of Pepperrellborough disappeared, replaced by the new town of Saco.

REV. JONATHAN EDWARDS, CLERGYMAN AND AUTHOR OF THE FAMOUS SERMON "SINNERS IN THE HANDS OF AN ANGRY GOD," visited Sir William shortly after Andrew's death. At that time, Edwards was the pastor of a church in Deerfield, Massachusetts, the site of the famous massacre of Queen Anne's War.

"To The Uttermost Of My Power"

In 1758, Edwards was elected president of The College of New Jersey in the small town of Princeton, five days after the death of his predecessor and son-in-law, Aaron Burr, Sr., father of the future vice president of the United States and duelist with Alexander Hamilton. Burr also had served at Louisbourg as a colonel of Connecticut troops.

Edwards was a popular choice for the college presidency, and he seemed to be a well-liked and competent leader of the fledgling college, but he died of smallpox only two months after taking office.

But before his passing, Edwards and New Jersey Royal Governor Jonathan Belcher -- former Massachusetts governor and friend of William Pepperrell -- persuaded the Baronet to donate liberally to the new college.

At about the same time, the Baronet was afflicted with a "painful ailment," diagnosed as probably a kidney stone, which was known to be extremely painful in passing. He apparently tried some remedies prescribed in various publications by a "Dr. Frankland" of Philadelphia, who, it seems, was Benjamin Franklin. The cure did not provide instant relief, as the Baronet hoped. He did not record an opinion of his new health care provider.

Another family tragedy struck in 1752 when Pepperrell's grandson -- Andrew Sparhawk -- died at age three. Andrew was not a lucky given name for the Pepperrell family.

Death certainly had an impact on William Pepperrell. He was a truly pious man, a man who believed God had direct impact on our lives through our direct actions. Like many of his contemporaries, he believed God

"To The Uttermost Of My Power"

actually took sides in mortal, earthly combat, much like the old Greek gods. No doubt he believed God fought with him against the French at Louisbourg and God had taken his son and grandson Andrew to a better place.

Faced with the loss of his son and heir, the Baronet now realized with finality his name would die out with his passing. This bothered him greatly. So he consulted with his lawyer, David Sewall of York, and came up with a solution.

But in the interim, more war blazed on the frontier horizon. The French and their Indian allies had not gone away. They still coveted the rich Ohio Valley, and many of them would still like to wipe the English colonies off the map. The governor-general in Quebec, and his new commander of regular French forces, the Marquis de Montcalm, had developed plans that, if properly executed, could give the French complete and final title to all of North America.[77]

In addition, the French again occupied Louisbourg, and new guns bristled from the freshly repaired ramparts of the Vauban-designed fortress. Merchant vessels and warships flying the white fleur-de-lis French flag filled its harbor once again.

The British too were tired of fighting for North America. For 50 years, the two sides had fought three wars that had decided nothing. It was time, felt many in Boston, New York, Philadelphia and London, to finally solve the situation.

---

[77] Parkman, Francis, *Montcalm and Wolfe*, p. 837-890.

"To The Uttermost Of My Power"

Once the forces moved toward the forks of the Ohio, war would not be far away. And Pepperrell -- the lieutenant general commanding at Louisbourg -- would be ready.

"To The Uttermost Of My Power"

Chapter XVII

"The Old French War"

IT WAS GEORGE WASHINGTON WHO BROUGHT WAR BACK TO THE AMERICAN COLONIES AND TO SIR WILLIAM PEPPERRELL.

Sent by Virginia's Lt. Governor Robert Dinwiddie to drive the French from the Ohio Valley, Washington blundered into a fight with the forces of the Most Christian King, Louis XV, and his Indian allies. In the resulting fight, the Americans killed a Gallic envoy, were trapped by the French at poorly located, poorly built, but properly named Fort Necessity, and had to finally surrender to the French who vastly outnumbered the Virginians. Washington and his men were allowed to return to their homes, but the French warned them to never return to the Ohio Valley territory.

These two men so vital to the history of British North America -- Washington and Pepperrell -- never met, although Washington admired Pepperrell, who after all had commanded at the largest British victory in the history of the colonies. By 1754 and his defeat in the Ohio Country, Washington's expressed desire was to receive a commission in the regular British Army, which was a goal he never achieved.

The war Washington started was the American version of the Seven Years War, known as the French and Indian War. It was the fourth and final of the colonial wars between the French and British in North America known collectively as the French and Indian Wars. Many referred to it as just "the old French War." Modern day historians do concede one thing about this clash of arms

"TO THE UTTERMOST OF MY POWER"

-- the Seven Years War was the first true "world war."

It was a war both sides knew needed to be fought. New France and the English colonies could not co-exist forever. Both sides wanted the entire continent for themselves, and each was determined to succeed. The British colonies had a much larger population, but they were limited in territory to a toehold on the eastern seaboard.

It was also during this time the people of these 13 colonies began calling themselves something other than colonists. Of course they were New Yorkers, Pennsylvanians, Georgians, etc., and they certainly did still live in colonial possessions. But more and more they became known simply as Americans.[78]

These Americans were surrounded by New France to the north, French forts in the Ohio region and Louisiana beyond that. The result of Washington's efforts on behalf of Virginia was to create the sparks needed to ignite the powder keg.

On the British side, the architect of the mad scheme of 1745 -- William Shirley -- was back in Boston as governor in 1754, having been on leave in Europe for several years and having never won his baronetcy. This time, Shirley proposed another scheme to the General Court, asking for funds to improve border fortifications in New Hampshire and Nova Scotia.

This proposal ran into some opposition, and among those against it was Sir William Pepperrell. The Kittery man felt that Massachusetts' defenses needed

---

[78] McCullough, David. *John Adams*, p. 41.

"To The Uttermost Of My Power"

improvement first, mainly because of the vast boundary the province -- especially Maine -- shared with many French outposts in that district. In fact, he had recently taken part in a conference with the Kennebec and Norridgewock Indians in an attempt to keep the border peace. Pepperrell argued that several forts should be strengthened, including Fort Richmond (Waterville, Maine) and Fort Western (Augusta, Maine), Falmouth (Portland, Maine), along with the Kittery harbor defenses.

Sir William won the argument on that issue, but Shirley got the authority to attack two forts that protected New France at the mouth of the St. Lawrence.

In 1755, Shirley and Pepperrell received authorization to reactivate their regiments (the 50th Foot and the 51st Foot respectively) from King George's War. But recruiting was difficult. As Pepperrell told Henry Fox (later Lord Halifax) in a letter, it was a simple thing to raise a volunteer Army, one that fights and then goes home. It is much harder to get men to enlist for twenty years as professional soldiers. Most colonists were farmers, homesteaders who favored fighting as militia.[79]

In that same letter, Pepperrell admitted to feeling some twinges of what he expected was a lingering illness. He told Fox: "I have been quite lame for some time now, occasioned not by a wound, but by great colds I got during the 49 days siege of Louisbourg, and living there the first winter after reducing it, before the houses were fitted up that we had shattered by our cannon and our mortars, but I feel daily I am recovering."[80]

---

[79] Parsons, Pepperrell to Henry Fox, February 23, 1755, p. 275.
[80] Ibid.

"To The Uttermost Of My Power"

In spite of recruiting problems, Britain resolved to bring the war to the French settlements in North America. General Edward Braddock brought a thoroughly British Army to North America, complete with drums and trumpets and those red coats that made such good targets in the American forests. Governor Shirley was named second-in-command of all British forces in the colonies, reporting to Braddock.

British strategy in 1755 called for a four-pronged plan of attack that included movement against the forts at the mouth of the St. Lawrence; a strike at Fort Duquesne on the site of present-day Pittsburgh; attacks on the Lake Champlain forts of St. Frederic (Crown Point) and Carillon (Ticonderoga); and expedition against Fort Oswego and Fort Niagara in western New York.

Pepperrell was expecting to take command of his regiment, the 51st Foot, as its colonel and lead it in action against the western forts. He and Shirley both had their regiments in the vicinity of Albany, New York, preparing for the movement toward the west.

Very unexpectedly, however, Pepperrell received notification that his old friend, King George II, had promoted him to major general in the regular British Army.

This elevation in rank entitled him to command much more than a simple regiment. The new rank meant he should command at least two brigades. A single brigade at that time in the British Army was usually composed of at least two regiments. Unfortunately, the British had more major generals than positions for them. In fact, Shirley, as second-in-command to Braddock, also became a major general with seniority over Pepperrell. There was no way the British could give the Baronet the

"To The Uttermost Of My Power"

command his status warranted. Braddock told Shirley he could not order Pepperrell to take just a regimental command, so the Governor asked the Baronet to take charge of the defenses on the eastern frontier of the colony. This order meant he would command if the French attacked the coastal towns amphibiously from the sea, something they had never done before. The Baronet went home to command in Maine.

MEANWHILE, BRADDOCK AND HIS ARMY -- including volunteer aide de camp George Washington -- marched on Fort Duquesne. The French and Indian defenders met Braddock's troops deep in the forest and inflicted appalling losses on the redcoats. Washington had three horses shot out from underneath him; among the British dead was William Shirley, Jr., son of the Governor. Braddock was mortally wounded and died on the retreat back to Virginia. His body was buried in an unmarked grave to protect the corpse from marauding animals.[81]

Next, General William Johnson, the Indian agent and nephew of the late Admiral Warren, was in command of the attack on the Champlain forts. Johnson led troops in the Battle of Lake George against a French Army under the Baron Deiskau. The battle was a tactical draw, although Johnson was able to garrison two forts in the area around the southern tip of Lake George -- the newly built Fort William Henry and Fort Edward.

With Braddock's death, Shirley now became general-in-chief in North America. He had finally reached his goal of commanding an Army, but, because he had no military experience, he proved to be an unfortunate choice.

---

[81] Flexner, James Thomas, *Washington -- The Indispensable Man*, p. 29.

"To The Uttermost Of My Power"

Shirley nevertheless wanted to prove his martial prowess. As part of the four-pronged attack on French possessions, he led his Army of British regulars -- including the 50th and the 51st - and colonial militia from Albany against a string of French forts in western New York. His final destination was Fort Niagara, at the site of the falls, but he was outflanked by a French force from Fort Frontenac, on the north shore of Lake Ontario. He could not advance toward his objective and by the time campaigning season was over, he had withdrawn a portion of his Army to Albany.

Although outmaneuvered in New York by the French, Shirley retained a British presence there by leaving 50th and 51st Foot regiments at locations along the southern shore of Lake Ontario. The troops themselves named the series of defensive sites -- Forts Oswego, Ontario and George -- collectively "Fort Pepperrell" in honor of the General who was left behind. Lt. Colonel George Mercer was in charge of the regiments in their respective defensive positions.

Fate, however, would not be kind to the men of the 50th and 51st Foot. Having wintered on the snowy lake, in 1756 they soon learned Shirley had been replaced in military command by a succession of generals including Daniel Webb, James Abercromby and finally John Campbell, the Earl of Loudon.

In order to concentrate strength, Lt. Colonel Mercer brought both regiments together at Fort Pepperrell, now known as Fort Oswego. In August 1756, the Marquis de Montcalm led an Army of French and Indians to the Great Lake and laid siege to Fort Oswego. Early in the action, a cannonball tore off the head of Lt. Colonel Mercer, throwing the defenders into confused terror.

"To The Uttermost Of My Power"

They decided to surrender to the gallant, honorable European Montcalm, who promised to release them on parole if they agreed to no longer fight.

The unarmed men were marched to Montreal, but along the route they were often attacked and butchered by roving Indian bands while their French guards merely watched. Hundreds died before they reached Montreal.

After the war, both regiments were disbanded and stricken from the British Army List. Their numbers were taken years later by other regiments.

THE YEARS 1755 THROUGH 1758 SAW THE REPUTATIONS OF MANY BRITISH GENERALS IN AMERICA GO UP IN SMOKE. Braddock, Shirley, Loudon, Webb and Abercromby, and to some extent William Johnson, all saw their military fame crumble under pressure from the French. The one man whose military stature did not decline was the man whom Shirley sent home. Later Sir William Pepperrell commented to his friend Peter Kenwood in England, "I have never been asked for military advice by General Shirley nor by any of the commanding officers of this war."[82]

It probably was too bad they had not sought his advice. Both before and during the war, he wrote to several friends advising more regiments like his and Shirley's should be created and have their ranks filled with Americans for service in America. Those soldiers would be trained in the ways of stealthy "forest fighting" to combat the similar ways of the French and their Indian allies.

---

[82] Parsons, Pepperrell to Kenwood, Feb. 7, 1758, p. 307.

"To The Uttermost Of My Power"

Writing again to Henry Fox in August 1755, Sir William noted "an army of these North Americans are, I conceive, the only fit men to meet a mixed army of French and Indians in the woods; at least in order for success, the English forces must consist of our New England officers and men who are acquainted with their manner of fighting and can deal with it."[83]

Pepperrell also added if Braddock's expedition had included several American regiments in his march to Fort Duquesne, the results might have been quite different and Braddock might have lived to fight another day.

Eventually, the British would learn the ways of forest fighting, and they would create formations such as Roger's Rangers and the Royal Americans, but it would cost many, many lives to drive those lessons home.[84]

GOVERNOR -- OR GENERAL -- SHIRLEY was not above using Pepperrell for his own purposes one final time. Shortly after the Battle of Lake George, Sir William Johnson resigned his commission, leaving the Champlain forts' attack group leaderless. Shirley asked the Baronet to recruit new troops for it, and the Kittery man saw this request as an offer of command.

But after Sir William had worked hard to raise the needed militia forces, Shirley gave the command to Lt. Colonel John Winslow. The veteran merchant/warrior from Kittery Point was livid and incensed by this latest bit of trickery, and finally he had enough of Shirley's duplicity. Usher Parsons wrote in 1856: "Pepperrell, had long known that Shirley was unfriendly toward him.

---

[83] Abatt, The Magazine of American History, p. 681.
[84] Ibid.

"To The Uttermost Of My Power"

Waldo had apprised him in 1748, as did the letters of Sparhawk. But not a word escaped indicating a corresponding feeling on his part until the command promised him against Crown Point was revoked. After which he held little or no further intercourse with him, except on official duties."[85]

Decades of controversy in Boston finally caught up with Governor William Shirley, however. King George II, on advice of the government, recalled him in September 1756 after nearly 16 years of service in Massachusetts. Baronet Pepperrell shed no tears on his departure.

King George then named Thomas Pownall to become the next governor of the colony. Born in 1722 and educated at Oxford University, Pownall first came to the colony of New York in 1754. One of his best friends was Benjamin Franklin, whom he met at a multi-colonial conference held in Albany that year.

Pownall strongly supported Prime Minister William Pitts' plans in the French and Indian War. After the war, Pownall and the other colonial governors fell increasingly under the control of the Board of Trade, the government panel that advocated increasing taxes on the Americans. As time went on, Pownall was unwilling to carry out their repressive policies to punish colonists, and he was discharged as Massachusetts governor in 1760. He was named Governor of South Carolina instead, but he never served there, however, and soon took a ship back to England.

Pownall held several military positions in Germany until the late 1770s when he returned to England to serve in

---

[85] Parsons, Pepperrell to Kenwood, February 7, 1758, p. 307.

"To The Uttermost Of My Power"

Parliament. During the American Revolution, Pownall generally supported the war to recover the 13 colonies.

With Shirley's departure, Lt. Governor Spencer Phipps was in charge during the interval until Pownall arrived in Boston. Phipps, however, died in March of the following year, leaving a power void at the government house. The next ranking official became acting governor and that was Council President Sir William Pepperrell. He served as acting governor for four months.

During this time, Sir William was installed as commander of Castle William, the military fortress in Boston harbor, and was given the ceremonial keys to the facility.

When Pownall arrived to take up his post, he went through a number of ceremonies designed to signify the transfer of power. Biographer Parsons noted: "When Sir William presented the keys (to Castle William), he (Pownall) observed that the fortress was the key to the province, which gave the governor the opportunity of complimenting the conqueror of Louisbourg. 'The interest of the province is in your heart; I shall therefore be always glad to see the keys of it in your hand.'"[86]

Meanwhile, the Old French War continued without cease. In 1757, the French and their Indian allies, commanded by the Marquis de Montcalm, captured Fort William Henry at the foot of Lake George (the Lake of the Holy Sacrement to the French), New York, and massacred the soldiers and camp followers as they marched out of the surrendered fort. James Fennimore Cooper immortalized this bloody incident in *The Last of the Mohicans*.

---

[86] Parsons, Pownall to Pepperrell, p. 298.

"To The Uttermost Of My Power"

The colonists throughout New York and New England now felt helpless with a victorious French and Indian Army on the loose in upstate New York. Many colonial leaders feared Montcalm would turn south toward Albany or east to Boston.

Governor Pownall now took action to protect his frontier and he turned to Sir William. Pownall wrote about his plans to the new prime minister in London, William Pitt: "Upon hearing that Fort William Henry was invested, I sent Sir William Pepperrell (whom I appointed Lt. General of the province) up to the frontiers to collect a body of Troops and send forward any reinforcements the situation should require."[87]

Pepperrell quickly traveled by horseback to Springfield, Massachusetts, in early August, where he took command of a rag-tag group of local militias. Shortly after his arrival, it became clear Montcalm had retreated north to Canada after destroying Fort William Henry and was of no more threat to the colonial settlements. His presence alone helped to calm down a frantic frontier.

When he was sure the threat was over, Sir William asked Pownall to release the troops and let them go home. It was late August, it was harvest time, and he knew the men would be eager to get back to the settlements to make sure their families had food for the winter. Pownall agreed with Pepperrell and the farmer/soldiers made it home in time for harvest.

Also in 1757, Lord Loudon, the new commander-in-chief, had plans to assault Quebec by sea and the St. Lawrence

---

[87] Rolde, p. 157.

"To The Uttermost Of My Power"

River. But Pitt told Loudon he could not take his Army down the St. Lawrence until he reduced the one location that would threaten his flanks and his lines of communication: Louisbourg. Once again in French hands, the Atlantic fortress was still a mortal threat to the British.

By the summer, Loudon had 6,000 troops in more than 100 ships in Halifax harbor waiting for the final word to move on Louisbourg. A small Royal Navy squadron under Admiral Edward Boscawen was also on hand as an escort.

Before they could leave Halifax, however, a large naval force from France suddenly appeared at Louisbourg, a fleet the Royal Navy squadron felt was impossible to beat. The British set sail for Boston, and Loudon and his army arrived back there safely. A portion of the Royal Navy squadron, however, was caught in an ocean storm that severely damaged a number of British ships before they could find safe harbor. Louisbourg stood secure again.

Prior to this second attempt to conquer Louisbourg, no British officer ever talked to Sir William about it, and he was the one man in the colonies who knew how it could be done. The next commanders would not make that mistake again.

Pepperrell didn't know it at the time, but the trip to Springfield would be his last campaign. Following the dismissal of the militia, he returned home to Kittery Point to his family, his friends and his business.

On his way home, Pepperrell realized how tired he was. He did not know what caused his fatigue -- was he getting too old; was it some remnant of the rheumatic

"To The Uttermost Of My Power"

fever; was it the business; or was it the aftermath of Andrew's passing? Whatever it was, the General just wanted to get home.

He also wondered if he would be forgotten by the powers in Boston and London.

The answer to the question came quickly and no, he was not forgotten. The new prime minister, William Pitt, was a good politician and an excellent war strategist. He was determined to end the strife in North America and to defeat the French once and for all. In order to do that, he had to find competent generals to lead the redcoats and the colonial forces. He found those officers in Jeffrey Amherst and James Wolfe.

Pitt didn't forget the Americans either. The prime minister gave Pepperrell yet another promotion -- to the rank of lieutenant general. It was the first time in British history a colonial-born officer had been so honored with such a high military rank. The promotion would be the last major honor of his life.

Things started to come full circle for Pepperrell. Generals Sir Jeffrey Amherst and James Wolfe paid a visit to Pepperrell at the Kittery Point mansion days before they set sail to besiege the strengthened fortress of Louisbourg. The Baronet was greatly pleased to be remembered by the Generals, and he spent hours with them recalling how his 1745 expedition reduced the fortress. The Baronet's old friend and comrade-in-arms, Samuel Waldo, had also briefed the Generals on the 1745 expedition.

Pepperrell no doubt was overjoyed when in the late summer of 1758, he heard Amherst and Wolfe successfully conquered Louisbourg a second time. This

"To The Uttermost Of My Power"

time it was totally destroyed -- it would no longer haunt New England.

In fact, Amherst's siege of Louisbourg followed much of the pattern set years earlier by Pepperrell. The British again landed at Freshwater Cove and established their camp at the same site used by the New England Land Forces. They also forced the French to abandon the Royal Battery, only this time the defenders did a better job of spiking the cannon before they left. Amherst set up a major battery at Lighthouse Point, which pounded the Island Battery into a useless pile of stone and mortar. Additional batteries soon were breaching the walls and destroying homes and other fortifications, and eventually the white flag of surrender again flew over Louisbourg.

The generals who visited the Baronet in Kittery achieved great fame in the final campaigns of the war. Although Wolfe died at the Battle of the Plains of Abraham outside of Quebec, his army won the battle and conquered the French fortress.

Amherst, as the commander-in-chief, won victories at Fort Ticonderoga and Fort St. Frederic (Crown Point) in 1759. Now the British finally took control of these massive stone fortifications on Lake Champlain. Amherst also laid siege to and conquered Montreal and accepted the final surrender of New France in 1760. He remained commander in North America until 1763. Amherst College and Amherst, Massachusetts were named for him.

Although Pepperrell had passed away before it took place, he, as the old Indian negotiator, would have watched with interest as the English tried to eliminate a major Indian threat from the north. It was a situation

"To The Uttermost Of My Power"

much like the one Maine settlers faced with Father Rale three decades ago. This time it was the St. Francis Indians who were causing concern along the frontier.

Named for their village and the Catholic holy man, the Abenaki Indians from the village of St. Francis along the St. Lawrence River had tormented border settlements, burning homes and stealing women and children. This time, the English were determined to end that threat.

In September of 1759, Major Robert Rogers and his Rangers crossed Lake Champlain from Fort Crown Point, hid their boats on the Vermont shore, and moved toward St. Francis. A French patrol found their boats and followed them, but the Rangers reached St. Francis before they did, and, in an early morning attack, destroyed the village.

The Rangers could not return to their boats as they had planned, so they split into smaller groups and moved east toward the remote Lake Memphremagog, and then on to the Connecticut River. Several Ranger groups were caught by the French and mercilessly slaughtered. But Rogers and most of his tired, starving men reached Fort No. 4 in Charlestown, New Hampshire, and safety. That raid ended the threat from St. Francis forever.

SIR WILLIAM PEPPERRELL WOULD MARCH TO WAR NO MORE. During the winter of 1758-1759, the rheumatic fever he had contracted after his return from Louisbourg came back to haunt him. He had never fully recovered from the attack in 1748, and now his age made him much more vulnerable to it.

He spent more and more time in bed, and he was rarely able to travel the 70 miles to Boston to handle his political duties. Doctors examined him and tried a

"To The Uttermost Of My Power"

variety of remedies, but nothing seemed to work. His friend Rev. Stevens and other ministers in the region prayed for his recovery. Lady Pepperrell prepared the family. But it was all done for naught.

The fever took his life on July 6, 1759 at Pepperrell Mansion.

"To The Uttermost Of My Power"

Chapter XVIII

A Life With Honor

THE PEOPLE OF THE PISCATAQUA RIVER REGION HAD NEVER SEEN ANYTHING LIKE IT BEFORE, AND THEY PROBABLY NEVER DID AGAIN IN THEIR LIFETIME. IN JULY OF 1759, THE REGION THAT HAD BEEN HIS HOME WAS ABOUT TO SAY GOOD-BYE TO THE LATE SIR WILLIAM PEPPERRELL, BARONET.

The Piscataqua communities would never see his like again. Other great men -- admirals, generals or politicians -- would come to the area to command for a while, but soon their service would be up and they would go elsewhere. Men like John Paul Jones and Admiral David Farragut would be but transient residents of the area.

No native son or daughter of the Piscataqua -- or even an adopted child -- ever rose as high as William Pepperrell.

By the end of June in 1759, the lord of Pepperrell Cove had been ill for some time. When Thomas Pownall, Shirley's successor as governor in Boston, had heard Pepperrell was bedridden, he made a special trip from Boston to visit the Baronet.

On May 4, 1759, *The New Hampshire Gazette* duly noted the Governor's arrival from Boston. He spent the night with New Hampshire Governor Benning Wentworth in Portsmouth and the next morning "went by his Excellency's barge to the seat of Sir William Pepperrell, Baronet. In Kittery, he received a handsome salute as he

"To The Uttermost Of My Power"

passed by the castle. We hear that Sir William lies ill at his seat at Kittery."

On May 30, Pepperrell was once again appointed to the Massachusetts Governor's Council. Noting this would be his 32nd year of consecutive service on that body, the council named him its president for the 18th time. The members in Boston knew he would never again take his seat, but they did it to honor him for the final time.

As time moved on, Pepperrell was confined to his bed and his condition continued to worsen. Doctors were brought to his bedside, but no remedy or medicine seemed to make any difference. Many friends who came to visit him left thinking they had seen the Baronet for the last time. Time itself was slipping away.

Two months after the Governor's visit, Pepperrell died quietly at his home. The cause of death was determined to be the lingering rheumatic fever he originally contracted eleven years earlier. But others claimed he had never gotten over the death of his only son and heir, Andrew, in 1751. A broken heart may have contributed to his demise.

Pepperrell's funeral service was held at his mansion in Kittery Point, the house his father built and which the Baronet turned into its current pre-eminence. The body lay in the first floor parlor, and Pepperrell's good friend, Rev. Benjamin Stevens of the Kittery Point's First Congregational Church, conducted the service.[88]

---

[88] Let me step out of the writer/historian's role for a minute. I could find no list of funeral attendees in my research; neither could several professionals whom I contacted at archival locations.

"To The Uttermost Of My Power"

Contemporary press reports said more than 300 mourners crowded into the mansion for the funeral. Hundreds of others lined the riverside. Grieving family members present included Lady Mary Pepperrell, his widow; Mrs. Elizabeth Sparhawk, his daughter, and her husband Nathaniel; the Baronet's grandchildren, including William Pepperrell Sparhawk, who had agreed to become William Pepperrell II on his grandfather's death; and his surviving sisters and their families.

Many civic leaders from throughout the Maine, New Hampshire and Massachusetts colonies were in attendance and extended their sincere sympathies to Lady Pepperrell and Betsy. Prominent members of leading Kittery families -- the Shapleighs, the Leightons, the Gunnisons, the Frosts and the Cutts -- crowded into the mansion to rub elbows with their counterparts from Portsmouth, including the Wentworths, the Gardners and the Warners.

Fellow merchants from the region and from Boston made their pilgrimage to honor Sir William. One person from this group was missing -- Pepperrell's old friend Samuel Waldo, who had passed away without warning in May. A variety of clergymen from other churches in the Piscataqua basin were there, as were members of militia units in their respective uniforms. British officers from Fort William and Mary also paid their respects. And something that would

---

But I wanted to give the reader an idea of what the funeral might have been like and who might have attended. So the next few paragraphs represent a brief foray into historical fiction. I certainly hope those mentioned did attend, but I have no way to prove that they did. Please forgive me for doing this, but one thought does give me comfort -- if they were not there, they should have been. The paragraphs are in italic.

"To The Uttermost Of My Power"

have pleased Pepperrell immensely happened when veteran soldiers he had led at Louisbourg also made appearances to bid farewell to their old commander.

There was a moment of excitement when the New Hampshire Governor's barge tied up at the dock and Governor Benning Wentworth, his brother Mark Hunking Wentworth and their families got off the vessel to pay their respects to Sir William.

As this was going on, flags on both shores of the Piscataqua River were lowered to half-staff as Kittery, Portsmouth and other regional communities honored his memory.

Church bells tolled in Kittery and Portsmouth, providing a ringing symphony to be heard on the river. They rang from the steeple of Portsmouth's North Church in Market Square, where Sir William was baptized; they echoed to the Anglican St. John's Church, high on a hill overlooking the New Hampshire shore of the Piscataqua River. The bells that rang at St. John's were captured at Louisbourg and donated to the church by Pepperrell. Those New Hampshire notes were answered in Maine by the bell at the Kittery Point Congregational Church, where Pepperrell himself had served communion to fellow parishioners not so long ago. Other Kittery churches joined in tolling their bells to honor the Baronet.[89]

As the funeral concluded, gun batteries on both shores fired lengthy salutes to mark the Baronet's passing.

---

[89] Frost, Joseph P., *Sir William Pepperrell: His Britannic Majesty's Obedient Servant of Piscataqua*, p. 28-30.

"TO THE UTTERMOST OF MY POWER"

Muffled drums rumbled in the distance as the funeral cortege made its way from the house to the nearby family tomb. There Sir William would join his late father and his late brother and son, both of whom were named Andrew.

Then Rev. Stevens said a short prayer, the casket was transferred to the stone tomb; the door was closed, and Sir William Pepperrell belonged to history. The tomb itself was something Sir William had ordered from London in one of his first acts in taking his brother Andrew's place running the Messrs. William Pepperrell so long ago.

Then the funeral was over, but it was not the last of the public accolades for Sir William.

On the Sunday following the funeral, Rev. Stevens rose in his pulpit and delivered a stirring sermon on his friend's great accomplishments.

Church going in the mid-1700's was a daylong affair, a marathon of sitting in hard wooden pews. The days of the thunderous religious revival in New England known as "the Great Awakening" and personified by the late Rev. Jonathan Edwards, were winding down and the brimstone might not have been as powerful as before, but there was still plenty of fire in the sermons. Services were hours long; some preachers were incredibly long-winded and enthralling. It appears Rev. Stevens was a more than adequate orator in his own right.

Rev. Stevens began his sermon by exploring, at length, the theology of death and what we must be prepared for when each of us face the Grim Reaper. Then he consoled Lady Pepperrell for her loss and provided a long litany of

"To The Uttermost Of My Power"

Sir William's accomplishments in business, on the bench, in the legislature and in command on the battlefield. His focus then turned to the little-known side of Pepperrell -- the personal side of the man.

> Nor was he who appear'd to such Advantage, and acquired such Honors in his publick capacity, less distinguishable by his engaging deportment in his private life. And as he had a high relish for the innocent and refin'd pleasures of society and friendship, so was the delight of his friends, and the life and spirit of every company. His honors were far from elating him with pride, as it is too commonly the case with little minds; but when arrived at his highest pitch, he treated all with that same easy freedom and condensation which had ever been esteemed so distinguished a part of his character.
>
> Attachment to his friends so firm as to be weakened by a change of circumstance or distance of time and place -- and his regards were extended to the descendants of those whom he had once lov'd and esteem'd . . . the friend, the acquaintance and the stranger that visited him, were always treated with great hospitality.

As he neared the end of his oration, Rev. Stevens could not ignore his friend's public life.

> HIS private affairs, though numerous and weighty, were far from engaging the whole of his attention; great part of his time was spent in the service of the public. He was early in life chosen to represent his town in the Great and General Court -- and sooner than is common among us, had a seat at the Board, as one of his Majesty Council, in which place of honor he was ever after annually elected, and which he fill'd in the time of his death, both which important trusts...he discharged with fidelity and honor, ever approving himself a friend to the interest and prosperity of the province.[90]

---

[90] Stevens, Rev. Benjamin A., *A Sermon Occasioned by the Death of Sir William Pepperrell*, Miscellaneous Collections, Massachusetts Historical Society.

"To The Uttermost Of My Power"

Lady Pepperrell was so pleased with the sermon she had copies printed based on a transcription of the Rev. Stevens original text. She then distributed copies of it to Sir William's friends and acquaintances.

The sermon was reprinted and published by newspapers throughout the colonies and especially in New England and New York. One reader in Virginia was said to have paid special notice to the remarks. He was a planter from the Potomac River region named George Washington.

NATHANIEL HAWTHORNE, IN HIS 1833 SKETCH OF PEPPERRELL, took one final look at the Baronet. He wrote:

> After the great era of his life, Sir William Pepperrell did not distinguish himself either as a warrior or a statesman. He spent the remainder of his days in all the pomp of a colonial grandee, and laid down his aristocratic head among the humbler ashes of his fathers, just before the commencement of the earliest troubles between England and America.[91]

This was an interesting -- if not erroneous -- look at Pepperrell's life after Louisbourg. He may have wanted an easier life after his return from London, but he did not get one. His son's death forced him back into the business world. He was active again in government, the law, business and other matters in spite of facing major tragedies. He did what he could to answer his colony's request for defensive action during the last of the French and Indian Wars, only to have that Janus of a friend, Governor Shirley, relegate him to a position of insignificance in Maine.

---

[91] Hawthorne.

"To The Uttermost Of My Power"

But Pepperrell did not live out the rest of his life in all the "pomp" speculated by Hawthorne. In letter and in deed, Baronet William Pepperrell looked out for his family, friends, and fellow colonists to the end of his days.

In life and in death, he was a colonial aristocrat and a true New England hero.

"To The Uttermost Of My Power"

Chapter XXI

Last Will And Testament

BARONET PEPPERRELL WAS A VERY WEALTHY MAN, AND HE HAD A VERY LONG LIST OF BEQUESTS IN HIS WILL PREPARED BY DAVID SEWALL, A LAWYER IN YORK, MAINE, A YEAR BEFORE HIS DEATH.

In drawing up the will, Pepperrell wanted to deal with three important issues.

First and foremost, he wanted to arrange for a comfortable widowhood for his wife of 38 years, Lady Mary Pepperrell.

In doing so, the will noted: "He gives to Lady Pepperrell half of his real estate, for her life; and the increase of all his livestock on all of his farms; his chariot, his chaise and her choice of two of his horses; all his wines and other liquors and one thousand pounds sterling." He also gave her the choice of four of his personal slaves, to be her property for her lifetime.[92]

His second objective was to provide for his family, especially his only surviving child, Betsy Sparhawk. His concern for her was heightened when her husband's

---

[92] William Pepperrell, Will, 11 January 1759, Miscellaneous Collections, Massachusetts Historical Society.

"To The Uttermost Of My Power"

firm, Sparhawk & Colman, recently entered bankruptcy. The Sparhawk bequest read as follows:

"To his son-in-law, Nathaniel Sparhawk, all the dividend to be allowed for his demand against the late firm of Sparhawk & Colman, and for his wife's and children's support, the income of the other half of his real estate, and the interest of one thousand pounds; also all his real estate in the north parish of York and Berwick; she being required to sign all receipts and to have the sole power bequeathed her legacy." She, of course, refers to Betsy Sparhawk.[93]

The Baronet was deeply concerned about the financial future of his daughter and son-in-law and no doubt this bequest was meant to help their situation. Pepperrell apparently did a good job of taking care of his widow and daughter. In the early 1760s, Kittery records listed the mother and daughter as the top two taxpayers, respectively, in the town.

With his surviving sisters, his generosity varied -- hopefully, they all married well. Sister Mary Prescott got 30 pounds; sister Miriam Tyler, received all rights to her home plus her home mortgage was paid in full; sister Dorothy Newmarch received debt forgiveness and six pounds; sister June Tyler was left 20 pounds sterling. The Baronet also forgave the debts of a number of kinsmen or left them small sums.

Next, he left twenty pounds sterling to his friend and pastor, Rev. Benjamin Stevens. To the poor of his parish Congregational Church, he left 200 bushels of corn annually, to be distributed by 50 bushel increments

---

[93] Ibid.

"To The Uttermost Of My Power"

through his executors and Rev. Stevens. Again to the poor of the church, he left ten pounds hard money annually, to be distributed by the minister and his executors.

Then the Baronet and his lawyer addressed his third and final concern -- the continuity of the Pepperrell name. In doing so, Sir William left small bequests or real estate property to all of his grandchildren -- with one exception. That was his second grandson, William Pepperrell Sparhawk.

In a pre-arranged agreement, the young Sparhawk was left the Pepperrell Mansion, the bulk of the estate, and the family business. In return, the grandson agreed to legally change his name to William Pepperrell II and all his male heirs would carry that name in perpetuity.

If William Sparhawk had been unwilling or unable to fulfill those terms, the bequest would go to the next oldest grandson. And so on and so on until you reached the oldest granddaughter. She would inherit if her HUSBAND agreed to assume the Pepperrell name. Sir William wanted to make sure the Pepperrell legacy survived into posterity.[94]

William Sparhawk was only 13 when his grandfather died. But he was more than willing to inherit all the money, property and the title of baronet. He agreed to the terms, changing his name legally in 1766 when he became of age. He became the second Baronet Pepperrell.

Sir William and his lawyer had done their job well.

---

[94] Ibid.

"To The Uttermost Of My Power"

Although the Pepperrell business died soon after the Baronet, it seemed that the family was reconstituted well enough to keep the family name alive. As Byron Fairchild wrote in his book about the family business: "about the only thing that could disturb it was a revolution."[95]

The Pepperrell business empire, built up for two generations, did not long last beyond Sir William. That business, like many others in all the thirteen colonies, ran full speed into the whirlwind known as the American Revolution 17 years after his death. The business died, however, because there was no logical person to run it. By the time the new William Pepperrell came of age in 1766, it was too late.

---

[95] Fairchild, p. 197.

"To The Uttermost Of My Power"

Chapter XX

The Fate of The Family

REVOLUTIONS ARE INCREDIBLY UNFEELING EVENTS. IF THEY TAKE PLACE SUCCESSFULLY, THE WINNERS TAKE ALL AND THE LOSERS ARE LUCKY TO ESCAPE WITH THEIR LIVES.

This was certainly true for the American Revolution -- one of the most bloodless and least violent revolts of all time. The losers in that contest were the Americans who remained loyal to King George III, the Loyalists.

Literally hundreds of prominent and not-so-prominent Loyalist families lost their land and their homes and fortunes to the Revolution. At the top of that list were the Pepperrell family of Massachusetts.

John Adams, a Boston lawyer and future president of the United States, once estimated that, during the War of the Revolution, one third of all Americans were Patriots, one third were Loyalists and the other third never chose a side.

Prominent among Loyalists during that period were William Franklin, son of Benjamin Franklin; Robert Rogers of Rogers Rangers fame; William Stark, brother of New Hampshire militia General John Stark; William Allen, chief justice of Pennsylvania; Chief Joseph Brant, chief of the Mohawk Indian nation; Oliver Delancey of New York and brother-in-law of the late Admiral Sir Peter Warren; Simon Girty, chief British Indian negotiator; and John Howe, publisher of *The Boston Gazette*.

"To The Uttermost Of My Power"

Pepperrell's descendants wanted no part of the New England Patriots and their desire to seek independence. They retained their strong allegiance to the Crown and disapproved of the violent tenor advocated by such groups as the Sons of Liberty.

In truth, it is hard to imagine Sir William Pepperrell working side by side and getting along with Patriot leaders like Samuel Adams or even John Hancock who, at least, would have been a commercial rival. He might have approved of Benjamin Franklin and George Washington before the Revolution, but he certainly would have abhorred John Adams and even Thomas Jefferson and their ideas of equality and democracy.

Old Sir William Pepperrell did not seem to have the soul of a revolutionary. Nor did the second Baronet Pepperrell.

William Pepperrell Sparhawk graduated from Harvard College in 1766, first in social ranking in his class. That same year, he became William Pepperrell II and took over the Kittery estate and mansion and what was left of the business.

In 1774, he was invited to take a seat on the Massachusetts Governor's Council, the body where his grandfather had sat for so long. He accepted the offer and from the beginning supported Governor Thomas Hutchinson as the colonial government tried to stifle the revolutionary zeal of the Sons of Liberty. When Patriot leaders demanded that the 35 members of the council resign to show their loyalty to the fledgling rebellion, Pepperrell was among the ten who refused. The Sons of Liberty now began to watch his every movement.

"To The Uttermost Of My Power"

The new Baronet loyally supported the Royal party throughout the incubation of the Revolution. Pepperrell was mentioned as a potential successor to the discredited Hutchinson when the official was recalled from Boston, but nothing ever came of it. When Lt. General Thomas Gage succeeded Hutchinson, he was made "military governor" of Massachusetts and one of the first things he did was to dissolve the General Court and the Governor's Council.

A realist like his grandfather, the young Baronet also saw the handwriting on the wall, and he didn't like what he read. While he was in Boston in late 1774, a York County congress of patriots, held in Wells, Maine passed two resolutions that interested the Pepperrell family. The first praised his grandfather, who had died 15 years before. The second, however, condemned William Pepperrell II as a Tory and a British sympathizer and proposed confiscating his property. Pepperrell never returned to Kittery.

At the end of 1775, well before independence, he was settled comfortably in London. On leaving Boston, Pepperrell's wife -- the former Elizabeth Royall of Boston -- caught a fever and died either aboard ship in transit or in Halifax, Nova Scotia. She was buried in the Canadian settlement.

Once Pepperrell's family arrived in London, the young Baronet and his family lived off money that had been kept on deposit going back to the days of the first William Pepperrell, and revenue from a plantation in Suriname in South America.

The extensive Pepperrell land empire -- built by the Colonel and the Baronet -- came to an end quickly, when

"To The Uttermost Of My Power"

it and most of the Pepperrell estate was confiscated, by what was now the Commonwealth of Massachusetts. It is believed to have been the largest single confiscation by any of the 13 newly independent states.

Pepperrell became a respected figure in the expatriate colonial community in England. After the Treaty of Paris was ratified and ended the war between England and the new United States in 1783, he sought a legal opinion to see if he could obtain compensation for or restitution of his American property and business. He was told the Massachusetts Confiscation Act of 1777 was final, and he and his heirs had lost all claim to what they had left behind.

William Pepperrell II died in London in 1816 at the age of 70. His only son, also William, had died without issue in 1809, effectively ending the Pepperrell line. The old Baronet's legacy work had all been for naught.

AFTER HER HUSBAND'S DEATH IN 1759, Lady Mary Pepperrell had a new home built about two miles down the road from the mansion so she could be nearer her daughter at Sparhawk Hall. The new home also was just across the road from the Congregational Church of Rev. Stevens, and she found much comfort in that. Her house and lands were confiscated along with the rest of the family holdings, but Lady Pepperrell was treated with great respect by the new government, which still honored the memory and accomplishments of her husband. They allowed her to buy back her home and property and never forced her to leave the Georgian-style house. She lived there for the thirty years of her widowhood. Lady Mary Hirst Pepperrell died peacefully on November 25, 1789.

"To The Uttermost Of My Power"

Lady Pepperrell also had the last word on slavery and how it impacted her family. In her will, she not only freed all of her slaves, but also left many of them with bequests of financial support until they could get on their feet as freed men and women.[96]

Son-in-law Nathaniel Sparhawk was an absolute Tory[97] sympathizer, but he died in 1776 in Kittery before Independence was declared. His wife, Betsy Pepperrell, stayed at Sparhawk Hall after his death, and watched as her sons all became Tories and all eventually left North America for England. Elizabeth Pepperrell Sparhawk died at Sparhawk Hall in September 1797.

Only her daughter, Mary Pepperrell Sparhawk, stayed in America. She became a Patriot, married a doctor and died in Portsmouth in 1815. Sparhawk Hall remained a private residence until it was finally torn down in the 1950s.

Although the old Baronet tried his best to prevent it, his family surname did die out with the adopted William Pepperrell II's son. The business was long gone, and all of the land the Colonel and the Baronet had so carefully collected had been seized by the revolutionary government and then redistributed. The Pepperrells fell victim to events like so many other families and

---

[96] Frost, p. 32.
[97] The lot of a New England Tory was not an easy one, mainly because after the British left Boston in March of 1776, they never returned. The American Revolution already was over in New England. For an excellent fictional look at the life of a Tory, see *Oliver Wiswell* by Kenneth Roberts.

"To The Uttermost Of My Power"

companies. Instead of being headliners in history like they were in the colonial era, the Pepperrells became footnotes in the history of the United States.

But the family name lives on with scattered pockets of relatives and in other ways as well.

The Town of Pepperell, Massachusetts, though spelled with one less "r", was named for Sir William.

Pepperrell Industries, a textile company, was founded in the 19th century on land once owned by the Pepperrell family in Saco, Maine. Although the company left New England with many other textile firms in the early 20th century and became known as West Point Pepperrell, the Pepperrell name was retained for many years as a brand of the company. That company merged with JP Stevens to form WestPoint Stevens, Inc.; it still uses the Lady Pepperell brand name for bedding products.

During World War II, the United States Army Air Force built a base in Nova Scotia near the city of Halifax. It was named the Pepperell Air Force Base; local residents called the entire complex Fort Pepperell. The base served well into the cold war years and was a key component of NORAD, the North American Air Defense Command. It closed in 1961.

Pepperrell property, however, remains newsworthy. In early 2007, Musician Darryl Hall -- of the duo of Hall and Oates -- paid more that $2 million for Kittery Point's Bray House, thought to be the oldest home in Maine and known to be the home of Sir William's mother, Margery Bray.

"To The Uttermost Of My Power"

Not far down the road is the Pepperrell Mansion itself, well maintained and well preserved in the 21st century. Many years ago, owners of the property removed about 10 feet from each end of the building, so it does not look like it did when the Baronet was still alive. It remains an impressive structure and home for its current residents. It is not open to the public.

The Lady Pepperrell House, built for the Baronet's widow, still sits in all its Georgian architectural glory at a 90-degree turn on Pepperrell Road, directly across from the First Congregational Church in Kittery Point. Several years ago, the house was listed for sale at a price of almost $2 million. There were no takers.

It is not open to the public.

Here is one final note about the family:

In 1745, William Pepperrell became the first American colonial figure to become a baronet. When William Pepperrell II was elevated to that same hereditary title in 1774, he was the last colonial to be so honored.

"To The Uttermost Of My Power"

Chapter XXI

The Passings Of The Era

THE 1760'S AND THE 1770'S WERE YEARS OF SLOW TRANSITION IN BRITISH COLONIAL AMERICA AS ONE GENERATION GAVE WAY TO THE ONE MATURING BEHIND IT.

Sir William Pepperrell had succumbed in 1759; his friend Samuel Waldo predeceased him in May of that year. Others followed, or preceded, Pepperrell, including, in no particular order:

- Adm. Peter Warren, 1751;
- Roger Wolcott, 1767;
- Col. John Bradstreet, 1774;
- King George II, 1760;
- Sir William Shirley, 1770;
- Gov. Benning Wentworth, 1770;
- Adm. Charles Knowles, 1777;
- The Duke of Newcastle, 1768;
- King Louis XV, 1774;
- Gen. Sir Jeffrey Amherst, 1797;
- Sir William Johnson, 1774;
- George Washington, 1799;
- Thomas Pownall, 1805;
- Louis, Marquis Duchambon, 1774;
- Marshal Marquis de Vauban, 1707;
- Robert Rogers, 1794;
- James Wolfe, 1759;
- Marquis de Montcalm, 1759;
- Hannah Waldo Flucker, 1777;
- Jonathan Belcher, 1757;

"To The Uttermost Of My Power"

- Edward Tyng, 1755;
- Benjamin Franklin, 1790;
- William Pitt the Elder, 1788;
- Richard Gridley, 1795;
- Rev. Benjamin Stevens, 1791;
- Seth Pomeroy, 1778;
- Elizabeth Sparhawk, 1797;
- Lt. Col. John Winslow, 1778;
- Gen. Henry Knox, 1805;
- Lucy Flucker Knox, 1826;
- John Adams, 1826;
- Thomas Jefferson, 1826.

"TO THE UTTERMOST OF MY POWER"

Epilogue

A True New England Hero

*I*T IS NOT AN EASY JOB TO TRY AND GET TO KNOW A MAN WHO DIED MORE THAN 250 YEARS AGO. THE PASSAGE OF TIME MAKES IT DIFFICULT TO UNDERSTAND THEIR THOUGHTS AND BELIEFS, THEIR WANTS AND DESIRES, THEIR FEARS AND SHORTCOMINGS.

But that is what biography is...getting to know someone through their own words and actions no matter how long ago they lived. I cannot truly say I got to know Sir William Pepperrell over the past few months, but I did get to know a lot about him. But maybe I did get to know him because as I write those words to end this work, I feel I am going to miss him.

He truly was a fascinating individual, one who came into the business world only because of the unfortunate death of his brother Andrew. In spite of his lack of commercial training, he turned his father's modest business into one of the great commercial empires in British North America. Then he became a successful land entrepreneur. He also served on the Massachusetts Governor's Council for 32 years, the last 18 as chairman. He was a learned jurist on the court of appeals, handling difficult legal cases with no formal training. He was a militia colonel whose responsibilities included what is now the entire state of

"To The Uttermost Of My Power"

Maine; he led the Army -- a New England Army -- that conquered the strongest fortress in North America; and he became the highest-ranking colonial to ever hold a commission in the British Army. He died a lieutenant general.

Through it all, he was a good man. It is difficult to find anything negative he said or was said about him. Most any negative comments made about him where based on jealousy of his success. Commodore Warren said some critical things about Pepperrell during the Louisbourg campaign, but Pepperrell never responded in kind. He could always raise troops due to his fine reputation and, being involved with cutthroat politics in Massachusetts, he was still known as a man of integrity and honor. He was a scrupulous jurist and an honest merchant.

He was a good husband, a good father and a good friend. He was almost too good to be true. He became a baronet and a lieutenant general, but he never lost the common touch that made him such a popular leader.

He will forever be linked to the 1745 siege of Louisbourg, which was the central event of his life, and which was one of the central events of his era. It showed the world and their British overlords the Americans had confidence in their abilities to fight and conquer the impossible, and it showed Pepperrell there were no limits to his abilities. It gave Provincials from New England an invaluable education in warfare and a military experience like no other at its time. It truly was a proving ground for many of the men who would fight the American Revolution. It is a shame that we have

"To The Uttermost Of My Power"

nearly forgotten the siege of Louisbourg and the man who led New England to victory there.

As one writer noted: "The greater names of Washington and the Revolutionary generals have now eclipsed that of Pepperrell, but it should not be forgotten that he did more than any other man to prepare the army that afterward achieved American Independence."[98]

I will close with the unfounded supposition, all my own, that if he had been a younger man and were so inclined and had conditions been right, William Pepperrell could have been the father of his country. An inexperienced George Washington was chosen as commander of the Continental Army because in 1776 his meager military skills were the best the Provincials had.

But William Pepperrell had already commanded an Army and successfully managed one of the most difficult things in military science -- an amphibious landing. He already knew how to organize an Army; he knew how to run a siege; he had the loyalty of his men. He would have known things at the outset of the war that Washington had to learn the hard way and with substantial loss of life.

If things had worked out, the Pepperrell Mansion in Kittery might be as revered today as Washington's Mount Vernon. And, to take things one far-fetched step further, the capital of the United States might be Pepperrell, D.C, in Maine, rather than Washington, D.C., straddling Virginia and Maryland

---

[98] Wilson, Fiske, Appleton's Cyclopedia of American Biography, p. 721.

"To The Uttermost Of My Power"

But conditions weren't right. Pepperrell was long dead and gone, by the time of the Revolution. His family and descendants were all Tories, and it is likely he would have been one too. Everything indicates he would have rejected the idea of independence from Great Britain. He was a man of the Crown, a true colonial, a man who understood his obligation to the King.

Still one wonders. Sir William certainly thought of himself as an Englishman, but England wasn't his home, America was. He had only been to England once, and he was very glad to get home. In his speech to the Massachusetts legislature on returning from Louisbourg, he did refer to New England as his home. In many ways, he was equally proud of being an American. Lady Pepperrell never left America, even though her house was confiscated; perhaps she would have convinced her husband to stay. Perhaps the lure of his life and lifestyle at Kittery Point would have been enough for him to support the Revolution. Perhaps he might have seen that it was time for the colonies to control their own fate and cast off the often-strangling oversight by Parliament, the Board of Trade and the British Prime Minister, not to mention the King.

He was, after all, a merchant and he and his business lived and died on paper, all kinds and sizes of paper. But paper was the target of the infamous Stamp Act of 1765. This act of Parliament was designed to help pay for the old French War by taxing every piece of paper used in the colonies through the use of stamps. The act caused huge protests, riots and recriminations before it was repealed. It might have been enough to turn a baronet into a revolutionary.

"To The Uttermost Of My Power"

Other attempts by Parliament to tax the American colonies without representation in the British legislature caused further problems in the provinces and could well have boosted any anti-British feeling that Pepperrell might have held. Like most merchants -- as well as most Americans -- he must have been horrified by what was called the Coercive Acts -- the series of orders that closed the port of Boston to all trade; revoked the Massachusetts royal charter; gave the colony a military governor and martial law; and sent 2,000 troops and three major generals -- William Howe, John Burgoyne and Henry Clinton -- to occupy the town of Boston.

Perhaps he might have protested against these injustices and joined the Patriot cause. His prestige was such that he might have attended the two Continental congresses with John and Samuel Adams as a Massachusetts delegate. Perhaps George Washington might have nominated Pepperrell to head the Continental Army. Perhaps his military background would have allowed the colonies to win their independence before 1783. Perhaps Pepperrell might have been at Yorktown, and perhaps he might have become the first president. Perhaps...one can only imagine the possibilities.

It is said that George Washington was a strong admirer of Sir William Pepperrell, having read a great deal about his taking of Louisbourg. When the first president visited the Portsmouth/Kittery area in November, 1789, he got out of his carriage and walked by Lady Pepperrell's house in tribute to the Baronet. When asked if he wanted to stop, Washington told the coachman no, muttering that he knew she would not receive him even if he did.

I think Washington was wrong. I think that Mary Hirst Pepperrell was an American first and a patriot or loyalist second. I think she had a mind of her own and she knew

"To The Uttermost Of My Power"

what she wanted. Apparently London did not appeal to her and Kittery did. She would not flee her home country and she had seen how the British treated her husband after Louisbourg and during the French war. She may have been proud to be an American and she might even have approved of President Washington. He should have knocked to find out.

Lady Pepperrell died peacefully at the end of that month.

"To The Uttermost Of My Power"

We will never know what Sir William thought about the Revolution, but we do have a fascinating and unusual glimpse of what it may have thought about him. In November of 1774, just five months before Lexington and Concord and with Sir William dead 15 years, a York County meeting in the Town of Wells, passed the following resolution:

> **The Late Sir William Pepperrell, honored in Great Britain and America for his eminent services, did honestly acquire a large real estate in this country, and gave the highest evidence not only of being a sincere friend of the rights of man in general, but of having a paternal love of this country in particular.[99]**

---

[99] Frost, p. 14.

Select Bibliography

Document Collections

The Pepperrell Papers, Massachusetts Historical Society, Boston, MA.

The Shirley Papers, Massachusetts Historical Society, Boston, MA.

The Pepperrell Collection, Portsmouth, NH, Public Library, Portsmouth, NH.

Books and Printed Sources

Abbatt, William, editor, *The Magazine of American History*, A. S. Barnes, New York, 1879.

Anderson, Fred, *The Crucible of War*, Vintage, New York, 2000.

Anderson, Fred, *The War That Made America - A Short History of The French and Indian War,* Penguin, New York, 2006.

Bourneman, Walter, *The French and Indian War: Deciding the Fate of North America*, HarperCollins, New York, 2006.

Brands, H.L., *The First American*, Vintage, New York, 2003.

Browning, Reed, *The War of The Austrian Succession,* St. Martin's Press, New York, 1993.

Chartrand, Rene, *French Fortresses in North America, 1535-1763,* Osprey, Oxford, UK, 2005.

Colonial Society of Massachusetts, *Publications of the Colonial Society of Massachusetts*, Boston, 1900.

"To The Uttermost Of My Power"

Cuneo, John, *Robert Rogers of the Rangers,* Fort Ticonderoga Museum, Ticonderoga, NY, 1958.

DeForest, L.E., *Louisbourg Journals, 1745,* Heritage Books, Westminster, MD, reprint 2004.

Demos, John, *The Unredeemed Captive,* Vintage, New York, 1994.

Eckert, Allan, *The Frontiersmen,* Little Brown, Boston, 1969.

Eckert, Allan, *Gateway to Empire,* Little Brown, Boston, 1993.

Eckert, Allan, *Wilderness Empire,* Little Brown, Boston, 1973.

Eckert, Allan, *That Dark And Bloody River,* Little Brown, Boston, 2000.

Edmonds, Walter D., *The Musket and The Cross,* Little Brown, Boston, 1968.

Fairchild, Byron, *The Messers William Pepperrell,* Cornell University, Ithaca, NY, 1954.

Flexner, James Thomas, *Washington: The Indispensable Man,* Little Brown, Boston, 1974.

Frost, J.W.P. and McIntire, Allyn, *Sir William Pepperrell: His Britannic Majesty's Obedient Servant of Piscataqua,* Newcommen Society, New York, reprint 1951.

Hibbert, Christopher, *Redcoats and Rebels,* Avon Books, New York, 1990.

Hunt, Freeman, *Lives of American Merchants,* "William Pepperrell", H.W. Derby, New York, 1858.

Leckie, Robert, *A Few Acres of Snow -- The Saga of the French and Indian Wars,* John Wiley and Son, New York, 1999.

Leckie, Robert, *The Wars of America,* Harper & Row, New York, 1968.

Maine Probate Abstracts, *Lady Mary Pepperrell,* Vol., 1, p. 993, Camden, Maine, Picton Press, 1991.

Maas, Peter, *The Terrible Hours,* HarperCollins, New York, 2001.

McCullough, David, *1776*, Simon and Schuster, New York, 2005

McCullough, David, *John Adams*, Simon and Schuster, New York, 2001.

McLennan, J.S., *Louisbourg: From Its Foundation to Its Fall*, The Book Room, Ltd., Halifax, Nova Scotia, 1979.

Miller, Nathan, *Broadsides,* John Wiley and Son, New York, 2000.

Middlekauf, Robert, *The Glorious Cause*, Oxford University Press, New York, 1986.

Parkman, Francis, *Count Frontenac and New France,* The Library of America, New York, 1983.

Parkman, Francis, *A Half Century of Conflict*, The Library of America, New York, 1983.

Parkman, Francis, *Montcalm and Wolfe*, The Library of America, New York, 1983.

Parsons, Usher, *The Life of Sir William Pepperrell, Bart. the Only Native of New England Who was Created a Baronet During Our Connection with The Mother Country*, University Michigan Press, Ann Arbor, 1856 Edition reprint.

Peckham, Howard, *The Colonial Wars*, Chicago, University of Chicago Press, 1964.

Pepperrell, William, et al., *An Accurate Journal and Account of the proceeding of the New England Land Forces During the Expedition Against the French Settlements on Cape Breton to the Ttime of the Surrender of Louisbourg* London, 1745, Massachusetts Historical Society.

Quinn, Arthur, *A New World*, Berkley Books, New York, 1994.

Randall, Willard Sterne, *George Washington, A Life,* Henry Holt and Company, New York, 1997.

Roberts, Kenneth, *Oliver Wiswell*, Doubleday, New York, 1976.

Roberts, Kenneth, *Northwest Passage*, Ballentine Books, New York, 1991.

"To The Uttermost Of My Power"

Rolde, Neil, *Sir William Pepperrell of Colonial New England*, Tilbury Press, Gardiner, Maine, 1982.

Rose, Ben Z., *John Stark, Maverick General*, Tree Line Press, Waverly, MA, 2007.

Shirley, William, *A Letter From William Shirley to His Grace the Duke of Newcastle*, James Parker, Esq., New York, 1746, Massachusetts Historical Society.

Steele, Ian K., *Betrayals: Fort William Henry and "The Massacre"*, Oxford University Press, New York, 1990.

Stevens, Rev. Benjamin, *A Sermon Occasioned by the Death of Sir William Pepperrell*, Privately printed.

William Pepperrell, Will, 11 January, 1759, Miscellaneous Manuscripts, Massachusetts Historical Society.

Wood, William, *The Great Fortress: A Chronicle of Louisbourg*, Hard Press, Quebec, Canada, 1915.

Williamson, William, *Sketches of The Lives of Early Maine Ministers*, Maine Historical Society, Augusta, Maine, 1896.

Zinn, Howard and Arnove, Anthony, *Voices of A People's History of The United States*, Seven Stones Press, New York, 2004.

Internet Resources

Answers.com, "Sir William Pepperrell", 2007

Google books.com, Howard. Cecil Hamden Cutts, *The Pepperrells In America*, The Essex Institute, 1906, reprint, 2008.

ElditchPress.com, Nathaniel Hawthorne, "Sir William Pepperrell", 2007.

Dictionaryof CanadianBiography.Com, "William Pepperrell", 2007.

EncyclopediaBritannica.com, "William Pepperrell", 2007.

"To The Uttermost Of My Power"

Wilson, James Grant, Fiske, John, eds, Appletom's Cyclopedia of American Biography, New York Public Library, 1893 edition.

Wikipedia.com, "Fortress at Louisbourg", 2007.

Wikipedia.com, "Sir William Pepperrell", 2007.

"To The Uttermost Of My Power"

Index

A

Abenaki, 20, 52, 59, 75, 223
Acadia, 61, 70, 81, 84, 86
Achilles, 180
Albany, 211, 213, 217, 219
Ambrose Gibbons, 15, 27
AMERICA, 4
AMERICAN REVOLUTION, xii, xviii, 32, 188, 217, 236, 237
Andrew Pepperrell, 191, 194, 195, 197
Andrew Sparhawk, 206
Annapolis Royal, 81, 82, 84, 104, 128

B

Baronet, 197, 225, 236, 250
Benjamin Franklin, 90, 205, 217, 237, 238, 245
Benning Wentworth, ix, 87, 92, 93, 136, 154, 172, 176, 185, 200, 225
Betsy Pepperrell, 241
Boscawen, 59, 220
Boston, ix, x, xv, 6, 22, 23, 25, 27, 28, 33, 34, 38, 39, 40, 41, 42, 43, 48, 49, 51, 56, 66, 73, 74, 78, 80, 81, 82, 83, 84, 86, 87, 90, 97, 102, 105, 108, 110, 133, 140, 142, 161, 167, 168, 170, 173, 174, 175, 180, 181, 182, 183, 185, 187, 188, 191, 192, 194, 195, 197, 198, 203, 207, 209, 216, 218, 219, 221, 224, 225, 226, 238, 239, 253, 254, 255
Brigantine *Kittery*, 43
Brooks, 125, 126
Brunswick, 8, 63

C

Canso, 29, 81, 82, 83, 103, 106, 107, 108, 112, 113
Canterbury, 132, 180
Cape Breton Island, xiii, 29, 70, 76, 81, 101,

102, 104, 105, 110, 128, 151, 154, 166, 185
Carillon, 71, 211, see Fort Ticonderoga
Coercive Acts, 249
Colonel William Pepperrell, 25, 27
Confiscation Act, 240
Congregational Church, 33, 46, 228, 235
Continental Army, xii, 196, 248
Count Frontenac, 58, 85

D

David Farragut, 225
David Sewall, 206, 233
DuChambon, 103, 104, 121, 122, 131, 135, 136, 137
Duke of Newcastle, 91, 106, 120, 139, 153, 155, 158, 166, 175, 253

E

Edward Braddock, 211
Essex, ix, 2, 180

F

Father Rale, 62, 63, 64, 65, 223
Fort Duquesne, 211, 212, 215
Fort Edward, 213
Fort Frontenac, 213
Fort Niagara, 211, 213
Fort Oswego, 211, 214
Fort Richmond, 210
Fort St. Frederic, 71, 175, 222
Fort Ticonderoga, 196, 222, 254
Fort William, 11, 34, 89, 145, 213, 218, 219
Freemasonry, 177
Freshwater Cove, 115, 222

G

Gabarus Bay, 107, 114, 119
General Court, 33, 41, 49, 60, 66, 75, 79, 82, 83, 84, 95, 97, 161, 168, 175, 185, 188, 189, 198, 209, 231
George Washington, xii, xiii, 196, 208, 212, 231, 238, 248, 250
Governor's Council, 83, 161
Great Britain, 1, 7, 8, 10, 31, 75, 86, 91, 148, 187, 248

H

Halifax, 210, 220, 239, 242, 255
Hannah Waldo, 193, 194

"TO THE UTTERMOST OF MY POWER"

Harvard College, 6, 41, 192, 238

I

Island Battery, 72, 113, 125, 127, 129, 131, 132, 133, 137, 138, 139, 222
Isles of Shoals, 13, 14, 16, 31, 167

J

Jeffrey Amherst, 116, 221
John Adams, 237, 238, 245, 255
John Bradstreet, 77, 87, 92, 117, 178
John Bray, 16, 17, 32, 33
John Nixon, 145
John Paul Jones, 225
John Wentworth, 53

K

King George's War, xiii, xvi, xvii, 5, 65, 187, 210
King Phillip's War, 33, 57
King William's War, 31, 58, 60
Kittery, xi, xiii, xiv, xv, xvi, xvii, 1, 3, 13, 16, 17, 20, 21, 22, 23, 24, 25, 26, 27, 28, 29, 32, 33, 34, 36, 39, 40, 43, 46, 48, 49, 50, 52, 57, 58, 65, 80, 88, 89, 97, 99, 133, 137, 147, 148, 170, 175, 178, 180, 185, 191, 192, 197, 202, 203, 210, 216, 220, 221, 222, 226, 228, 234, 238, 239, 241, 243, 248, 249, 250
Knowles Riots, 182

L

Lady Pepperrell, xv, xvi, xviii, 172, 195, 202, 230, 231, 233, 241, 243, 249, 250, 251
Lake Champlain, 71, 86, 175, 211, 222, 223
Lake George, 145, 212, 216, 218
Lake Memphremagog, 223
Lighthouse Point, 127, 222
Long Wharf, 168, 181
Lord Loudon, 219
Louis XIV, 10, 58, 69, 70
Louis XV, 10, 103, 143, 173
Louisbourg, x, xiii, xvii, 1, 2, 3, 5, 6, 69, 70, 71, 72, 73, 74, 76, 77, 81, 82, 83, 84, 86, 87,

"To The Uttermost Of My Power"

89, 91, 92, 97, 98, 99,
102, 103, 104, 106,
107, 108, 110, 112,
113, 114, 120, 122,
124, 125, 127, 130,
131, 132, 133, 135,
136, 137, 138, 139,
140, 141, 143, 144,
145, 146, 148, 149,
150, 151, 152, 153,
154, 156, 157, 158,
159, 160, 161, 162,
163, 166, 168, 169,
172, 173, 174, 177,
178, 179, 180, 183,
184, 185, 186, 187,
188, 189, 191, 205,
206, 207, 218, 221,
222, 224, 228, 232,
247, 250, 253, 255,
256, 257
Louisiana, 202, 209

M

Mad Scheme, x, 77, 78,
82, 87, 102, 147, 148,
170, 209
Maine, xi, xii, xiii, xiv,
xv, xvi, xvii, xviii, 1, 6,
11, 13, 15, 16, 20, 21,
24, 26, 27, 28, 32, 33,
34, 38, 45, 49, 51, 52,
56, 58, 67, 77, 78, 81,
84, 91, 105, 106, 174,
175, 185, 186, 196,
203, 209, 212, 228,
232, 233, 243, 246,
248, 256
Margery Bray, xvi, 17,
27, 243
Marquis de Montcalm,
75, 206, 214, 218,
244
Mary Hirst, 38, 39
Massachusetts, ix, xii,
xiii, xv, xvii, 1, 16, 21,
22, 33, 38, 49, 52, 53,
56, 59, 60, 61, 66, 74,
78, 79, 80, 84, 87, 92,
95, 105, 117, 145,
148, 156, 157, 161,
170, 171, 185, 186,
188, 193, 205, 209,
217, 219, 223, 225,
237, 238, 240, 242,
246, 247, 250, 253,
254
Merrymeeting Bay, 63
Montreal, 55, 71, 86,
214, 222

N

Nantasket Roads, 180,
181
Nathaniel Meserve, 123,
176, 177
New England, x, xiii, 2,
6, 11, 18, 30, 39, 41,
52, 55, 56, 57, 74, 76,
77, 79, 80, 81, 82, 86,
87, 89, 91, 92, 99,
100, 102, 103, 105,

111, 119, 126, 133, 134, 136, 137, 141, 142, 143, 152, 154, 159, 161, 166, 167, 169, 173, 174, 175, 188, 201, 203, 218, 222, 229, 231, 238, 242, 246, 247, 253, 256
New France, 54, 55, 56, 58, 61, 74, 75, 84, 85, 103, 209, 210, 222
New Hampshire, xv, 11, 13, 21, 22, 24, 26, 33, 34, 53, 56, 58, 77, 87, 92, 93, 94, 95, 107, 110, 122, 123, 154, 171, 185, 186, 200, 209, 225, 228, 237
Newfoundland, 15, 17, 27, 28, 31, 70, 73, 74, 104, 178
Norridgewock, 62, 63, 209
North Carolina, 28, 31
Nova Scotia, 61, 81, 84, 178, 201, 209, 239, 242, 255

O

Ohio, 56, 206, 207, 208, 209
Ohio Valley, 208

P

Patriot, 145, 195, 238, 239, 241, 250
Pepperrell Fleet, 25, 31, 38
Pepperrell Mansion, 30, 43, 193, 224, 248
Pepperrellborough., 204
Piscataqua River, xiv, xvi, 11, 15, 20, 21, 22, 66, 225, 228
Plains of Abraham, 222
Portsmouth, ix, xiv, xv, 13, 14, 17, 21, 22, 23, 24, 26, 29, 33, 43, 44, 74, 77, 87, 123, 133, 154, 167, 171, 176, 185, 196, 200, 225, 228, 241, 250, 253
Portsmouth Naval Shipyard, xv, 14, 24

Q

Queen Anne's War, 61, 70, 89, 104, 205

R

Rev. John Newmarch, 33, 43
Rev. Jonathan Edwards, 205, 229
Rev. Samuel Moody, 38, 91, 140
Richard Gridley, 145

Roger Wolcott, 95, 106, 157
Rogers Rangers, 237
Royal Battery, 116, 117, 118, 124, 125, 222
Royal Navy, 147

S

Samuel Adams, 183, 238, 250
Samuel Waldo, 5, 6, 46, 47, 50, 77, 79, 96, 106, 155, 157, 174, 193, 221, 228, 244
Seth Pomeroy, 145
Seven Year's War, 208
Sir William Pepperrell, i, x, xvi, xviii, 7, 100, 186, 208, 209, 214, 218, 219, 224, 225, 226, 229, 238, 246, 250, 254, 255, 256, 257
Sir William Phips, 84
Sparhawk & Colman, 46, 161, 192, 234
Sparhawk Hall, 46, 240, 241
St. Francis, 223, 224
St. John's Church, 33, 228
Stamp Act, xviii, 51, 249
Stephen Minot, 194

T

The 50th Foot, 147, 210
The 51st Regiment of Foot, 147
The Baronet, see Sir William Pepperrell
The Colonel, 28, 29, 30, 31, 32, 33, 34, 41, 42, 43, 242
The Last of the Mohicans, 218
Thomas Cushing, 168
Thomas Flucker, 194
Thomas Hutchinson, 239
Thomas Pownall, 217, 225
Treaty of Aix-La-Chappelle, 5, 187
Treaty of Paris, 240

V

Vigilant, 124

W

War Council, 95, 106, 121
Warwick, 180
William Johnson, 109, 180, 212, 214, 216
William Pepperrell, see Sir william Pepperrell
xii, xvi, 6, 14, 17, 26, 27, 32, 35, 36, 37, 42, 45, 46, 48, 53, 54, 66, 74, 78, 79, 80, 81, 88, 93, 151, 172, 183, 187, 191,

197, 201, 206, 216, 225, 232, 235, 238, 240, 241, 248, 254, 256, 257
William Pepperrell II, 238, 240, 241
William Shirley, ix, xvii, 49, 51, 67, 76, 78, 79, 91, 98, 155, 209, 216, 253
Wm. Vaughn, 77, 87, 92, 107, 116, 125

Y

York, 11, 28, 32, 34, 38, 39, 50, 51, 52, 58, 59, 65, 66, 73, 74, 79, 91, 93, 96, 109, 142, 145, 158, 173, 180, 196, 203, 206, 207, 211, 213, 217, 218, 231, 233, 234, 237, 253, 254, 255, 256

www.ingramcontent.com/pod-product-compliance
Lightning Source LLC
Chambersburg PA
CBHW070727160426
43192CB00009B/1351